Dear

Thank you for all you've done for me! I really appreciate your positive review.

Sincerely,
Jim Weihrouch

The Lean and Agile Home

A Bachelor's Journey

Jim Weihrouch

Published by Full Sail Publishing
Chicago, IL

ISBN: 978-0-9910823-8-4

For Lauren, who has made my life better in countless ways.

CONTENTS

Grateful acknowledgment is made to the following people who allowed me to reprint or reference their previously published materials:

Lean Dimensions figure (first appearance in chapter 2): Permission granted Niklas Modig and Pär Åhlström. (Figure was modified from their book This is Lean).

Cynefin® framework (first appearance in chapter 4): Permission granted from Dave Snowden. (Cynefin framework figures were modified from several references.) Cynefin is a registered trademark of Cognitive Edge.

The Yerkes-Dodson Stress and Performance Curve (chapter 8): Permission granted from Daniel Friedland, MD. (Figure was modified from his book Leading Well from Within)

Preface

I ran a household of one for many years. During this time, I worked in technology development, which required working long hours. Over time, the hours got longer as companies strived to do more with less in an era of globalization.

I often took early-morning or late-night conference calls to talk with people in Europe or the Far East. I would also send emails to coworkers in Europe before midnight, already the morning of the next day in Europe, to get answers by the time I started working the next day in Chicago. Fun, it wasn't.

At times, I wondered if I might have been better suited to be an artist rather than an engineer. As I worked, I saw hints of my artistic nature here and there. I always took time and care to make the slides in my technical presentations look nice, striving to make the technical slides have symmetry, scale, and color coordination. This was so unusual in my profession that, early in my career, my director told me I might have missed my calling as an artist despite an upsetting memory from elementary school.

My second-grade teacher was unpleasant and not supportive of my budding creativity. While I sat at my desk, working on an assignment, the teacher walked by and saw the way I signed my name at the top of my paper. This was my signature style, the way I had always printed my name in the second grade:

"Why do you write your name that way?" my teacher asked. "Do you want to be called Jim Smokestack?"

I looked up at her annoyed face and pursed lips as she hovered over me, and then stared back at my paper. I was speechless, my young artistic heart crushed. I never again put the puffs of smoke above the "i" in my name. Until now!

Writing this book has allowed me to tap into my artistic side. The more I thought about it, the more I realized how much of my approach to home maintenance comes at things from a creative approach as well as a technical one. This gave me one "why" for writing this book.

A second "why" for writing this book is that the concepts and examples about running a household I'll share with you are ones almost everyone should know because they are useful at home and at work. They'll give you a good starting point and guide for making your own home efficient, and they will show you that there are seldom rigid rules for how to go about it. As you'll learn, it's best to be flexible and creative in your approach to handling things around your place.

Lean and the Cynefin Framework

We'll talk about running a "lean" household, a practice you might be familiar with since many businesses are striving to become leaner, and you might have run into this at work. For our purposes, you'll learn that lean is about more than saving resources. There is another dimension to it—time—which is explained in chapter two. You'll also find there are times when lean concepts can be taken too far. It is difficult to apply lean concepts to anything that changes a lot. When it comes to your household, many things will stay the same, and some will change over time.

To make sense of all this, we'll talk about the Cynefin framework. This framework makes sense of situations or problems by characterizing them and approaching the problem depending on how it is characterized. When it comes to your home, a framework like this allows you to creatively engineer the best responses to emergencies as well as develop the best way to approach day-to-day tasks.

Sustainable

Woven throughout the book are tips on how to make a home more sustainable. Running one household effectively won't change the world, but it can give you more time and energy for other things in your life and bring you a sense of well-being. If everyone collectively ran their households even a bit more sustainably, it would make a huge difference.

These ideas and tools might help you at work too; applying them in your household will spark ideas you can apply in other contexts.

Fun

You'll see I've drawn the figures myself, many by hand. Some of the figures are for fun, and other figures are used to help explain complicated concepts. Drawing and writing this book put me back in the right universe while offering a fun yet practical approach to running a household that anyone can benefit from.

I love to learn and to understand how things work—whether those things are machines, complicated technical systems, organizations, or larger systems composed of people. I love to explain concepts I've learned but find it more fun for everyone if I do so in a lighthearted and memorable way. So, I hope this book brings you a few smiles and laughs as you formulate your best household management plan. We can all use that.

1

Bachelor Household Management

Running a household takes time, energy, perseverance, focus, spirit, and courage. Running a household alone takes all these attributes, times two.

As a bachelor, I lived in apartments and in a single-family home. My first experience with homeownership was a single-family, 1950s ranch-style house in a suburb of Chicago. There was a semi-finished basement, giving me plenty of room to store tools and raw materials needed to engineer and build my house projects. A third of the basement had vintage knotty-pine paneled walls and dark-green speckled tile. A closet with knotty-pine doors held cans of remnant house paint from over a half-century.

Shortly after moving into my house, I met an elderly

gentleman who had owned his home for decades. "You build a house, and then nature works to tear it down!" he said. His hearty laugh expressed his playful yet slightly cynical views on homeownership.

At the time, I didn't fully appreciate his wisdom. But now, after years of living in different homes, I realize the numerous threats nature and time pose to one's home.

My first house was constructed completely of wood, which compounded maintenance issues. There was always peeling paint or exposed wood somewhere on the house that needed painting. The extreme Chicago weather constantly wore away at the outside of the house. When I bought the house, I hadn't considered the interior walls and the paint they would need or the impact of small animals that took up residence in my attic. The myriad equipment inside the house—furnace, hot water heater, and several major appliances that needed to be maintained—hadn't occurred to me either. All these things went over my head during my conversation with the wise, old sage. Flush with the newness of homeownership and an engineering background, I was certain I could handle anything my new house threw at me, despite what my neighbor said. I can still see him laughing in my mind.

Many engineers think they should be able to fix anything. Others say, "Never let an engineer fix anything!" I fell somewhere between the two extremes. My first inclination when issues arose around the house was to assess the problem to see if I could fix it myself. I still do this. I am an engineer! But over time, my many failed repair attempts have humbled me.

A lot of engineering involves figuring out how to get something done for the lowest cost. One of my engineering professors worked in the auto industry in the late 1970s. Early in his career, he told the class, an engineer would redesign a muffler to save a dollar. That seemed far-fetched to me until I started working as an engineer. I worked on teams where we designed electronic circuitry that cost thousands of dollars per copy to build. Every part, whether it cost three cents or three hundred dollars, was scrutinized. When making things by the thousands or millions, costs add up. The same can be true for home maintenance; little costs add up to big ones.

Once, in a large, multi-story office building, I noticed the size of the bathrooms on the upper floors were the same as the bathrooms on the lower floors. Nothing unusual about that. But there were fewer offices on the upper floors and fewer people. Still, in the upper-floor bathrooms, there was space and plumbing for the same number of sinks as on the lower floors, but half of the sinks were missing in the upper floor bathrooms, leaving only capped pipes sticking out from the walls. Some engineer had figured out a way to save a few bucks by installing fewer sinks!

While I worked as an engineer in these cost-conscious environments, this way of thinking spilled over into how I ran my household. When I coupled my analytical side with my inner creativity, I realized running a household or a business, or living life, is as much about philosophy as it is about anything else. Success is about values and choices. Hopefully, these values and choices are made consciously and with some deliberation, especially the important ones.

While I titled this chapter "Bachelor Household Management" and refer to bachelors in this book, the ideas I present apply to anyone running a new household on their own or who finds themselves in charge of their first place, tasked with making things run smoothly.

Household Decisions

There are some basic decisions you need to make about your household. These decisions are important because they set the tone for your home environment, including cleanliness, tidiness, comfort, and the overall impression your place will make on you and others. These easy decisions are a good starting point in your home management journey.

Some of the most basic decisions are:

- Are you going to have a "shoes-on" or "shoes-off" home? How about your guests? What about during parties and social occasions at your place?
- Will you or your guests use coasters?
- Will you wash your dishes after every meal?
- How often will you clean (floors, bathrooms, food scraps, dust, dirt, and grime)?
- Will your place be organized, straightened-up, and tidy?
- What kinds of food will you stock, and how much will you keep on hand?
- Will you try to eat healthily and pay attention to balance and nutrition?
- Will you eat out all the time, order in, or cook?

- Will you have fancy pots and pans for specialty cooking or just the basics?
- Will your home or parts of it always be ready for guests?
- Will you take care of your own laundry and arrive at social occasions or your job in wrinkle-free clothes, or will you give a rumpled impression?
- Will you live as sustainably as possible, minimizing resource usage and maximizing recycling?
- Will your household have productive capacity (e.g., tools to repair, install, create, and maintain) or only consumptive capacity, relying solely on outside contractors?
- If you currently don't have home-maintenance skills or knowledge, what type of do-it-yourself projects (mechanical, electrical, plumbing, woodworking, landscaping, gardening) do you want to tackle?
- What resources (time, money, tools, machinery, vehicles) will you use or optimize?

My choices reflected my desire to make my home care as easy as possible. I decided on a shoes-off policy for everyone in the house that I maintain to this day. This practice keeps your place as clean as possible and will reduce the time you'll have to spend cleaning the floors.

I always use coasters on wood surfaces, so I don't create those white rings that can be impossible to remove from some furniture.

I have more pots and pans than I need but rely on a saucepan and a frying pan.

As a bachelor, my home was never ready for guests.

Then and now, I try to live as sustainably as possible, and I invested in tools that allowed me to tackle home projects myself.

Being an engineer, I assume I can fix many things. One of my first paychecks went to purchasing a Craftsman tool set that included an assortment of wrenches, screwdrivers, sockets, and other tools. I have steadily grown my tool collection and repair skills over time. I'd suggest you purchase the basics, at minimum—a hammer, screwdrivers (a Phillips head and a flat head), an adjustable wrench, and pliers. And, of course, duct tape.

I love it when I can fix something easily, and then proudly say, "See what I did!" Not all repairs I tackled fell into this category. Some repairs were successful but took more time and effort than they would have taken a professional.

I've also made repairs where I thought, "I shouldn't have done that," usually in the middle of a particularly challenging situation. Other repairs ended up as complete failures, I even made some problems worse with my efforts.

Some projects fall into the category of "I'm not even going to attempt that." For me, this category has grown over time. After several attempts, I've realized I'm terrible at plumbing. The old pipes in my 1950s ranch house didn't help.

For safety reasons, I always have experts work on natural-gas piping and most electrical repairs. Unless you are a professional plumber or electrician, I recommend you do the same. Knowing theoretically how something works doesn't equal having the skills to fix it safely. The most important knowledge to have is of your own skill level.

When making one of the many decisions to make around your home, act consciously and deliberately, establishing your own standards to create a living space you feel comfortable in.

It's best to develop efficient methods of dealing with household chores like doing the dishes and the laundry. Since these are the most repetitive chores around the house, figuring out efficient ways to deal with them will save you a lot of time and effort.

Before diving into the how-to part of efficient and lean ways of doing things, let's dive into some theory surrounding best practices to give ourselves a frame of reference as we proceed.

2

What is Lean?

"There is nothing more practical than a good theory."
Kurt Lewin

Before getting into the nitty-gritty of how I operated my household in a lean way, we need to establish what "lean" means.

Many businesses use lean techniques to eliminate waste and increase profits by minimizing costs and maximizing output. I used to think lean just meant reducing material and energy waste, along with eliminating steps that don't add value to the final product or service. What is often missed is that lean also involves how quickly something is done.

I've learned the most about lean concepts from *This is Lean: Resolving the Efficiency Paradox* by Niklas Modig and Pär

Åhlström. If you'd like to take a deeper dive into this subject, see Modig and Åhlström's book. For now, let's look at how these concepts tie into managing a home.

What is "Lean"?

Lean consists of two dimensions. One dimension is how efficiently resources are used. The other dimension is time efficiency. The following figure shows the dimensions of lean on a graph.

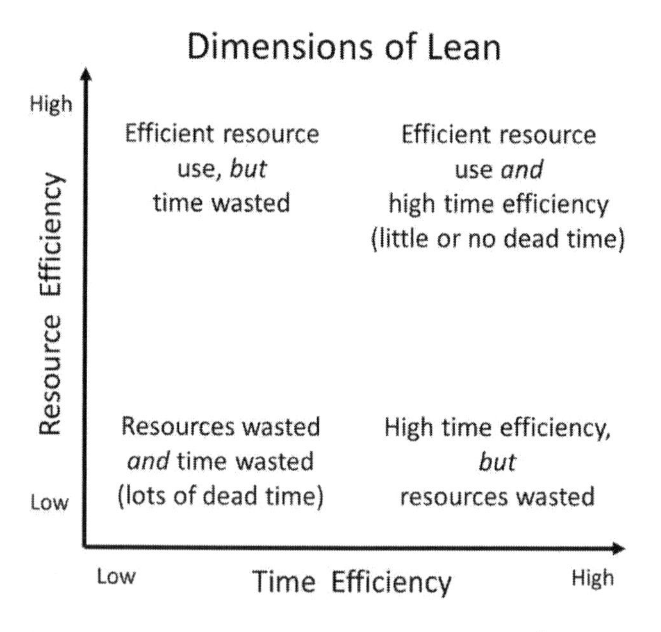

Adapted from "This is Lean," by N. Modig, P. Åhlström

Resource efficiency is what it sounds like—how efficiently resources are being used. Examples of resources are money, energy, materials, and labor.

In a bachelor household, labor relates to the effort it takes to complete tasks or chores. Effort is one of your most precious resources. If you wash dishes and use four times more labor, water, and soap than you need to get the job done, your resource efficiency is 25%, clearly not a good use of your energy and resources.

Time efficiency measures actual work time as compared to the total time it takes to complete a project. For example, washing pots and pans might take ten minutes of actual work. But, if in the middle of the job, you decide to watch TV for ten minutes, the pots and pans are worked on for ten minutes, but the job takes twenty minutes to complete. You've spent ten minutes loafing. This makes the time efficiency of this job 50%. Your ten minutes of loafing could also be referred to as dead time with respect to getting the dishes done.

Stick with me here; this simple shift in the way you approach household tasks has the power to add time to your day (something we all can use). But first, you must understand the concept.

The efficiency of completing a task can be categorized in one of four ways. When looking at the Lean Dimensions figure, these four ways are:

- In the lower left is **low resource efficiency and low time efficiency**. Resources are wasted, and time is wasted (there is a lot of dead time).

- In the upper left is **high resource efficiency and low time efficiency**. Resources aren't wasted, but time is wasted.

- In the lower right is **low resource efficiency and high time efficiency**. Resources are wasted, but the job is done quickly (there is little or no dead time).

- Finally, in the upper right, is **high resource efficiency and high time efficiency**. Whatever is being worked on is completed with only the needed resources (little or no waste), and there is little or no dead time.

The categorizations in the Lean Dimensions figure are the extremes. When doing something or contemplating how lean the work is, tasks can fall anywhere on the diagram, not just at the extremes. Many things we do fall into those gray areas, in-between extremes. This is especially true when more than one person handles tasks.

In our jobs, many of us have seen work move between departments in an organization. The goal of each department might be to ensure people and machines in their department are busy (no wasted labor or machine time). The busy department exhibits resource efficiency and can say to their management, "Look how efficient we are!" If you measure the department's success in isolation, things look great. But not so fast.

Often, work piles up before entering the department or waits inside the department until people get to it. Time passes (dead time) while the incomplete work pauses. So, although there is high resource efficiency, the time efficiency of the department is low.

Why can't everything be done with high resource efficiency and high time efficiency? Modig and Åhlström identify variation as the reason why this perfect state is hard to achieve. Picture a perfectly designed auto assembly plant where all the parts arrive just-in-time, and workers assemble them at the perfect moment as the auto moves along the conveyor. Many of us have seen video clips of factories like these. Variation has been designed out of the assembly process, so there is little resource or time waste. This is seldom the case at home. And, don't worry, I'm not making a case for trying to automate your household tasks to this degree. But I am saying that the closer you can get to this state of perfection, the easier and leaner your household tasks will become.

Most tasks in your home or at work are not so perfectly orchestrated because there is variation all around us. The ideal—resource and time efficiency—is difficult to achieve because of this variation. But with a few tweaks and an eye for the lean, you can come close, resulting in better use of materials and labor, less waste, and more time to enjoy other things in life.

When striving to make a task as lean as possible, consider your goals. How well and how quickly does the task need to get done? Look at the task and your goal a few different ways to find your best solution. For example, it takes less effort to dump all your clothes in one laundry load, but your white shirts will turn a gray color after a few loads—this doesn't meet laundry quality criteria, so you'd be better off taking the time to separate your clothes into smaller loads. If you decide to do dishes once a week, and you're okay with having lots of unwashed dishes around, then low time efficiency for this task is okay. Leaving the dishes undone for a time might allow you to focus on a more critical task.

These quality and timeliness decisions are worth considering as they set the philosophy for running a household. Now, let's look at a few more choices you'll have to make.

The Labor-Money Trade-off

In running a household, your labor (including your attention) and your money are two of your biggest resources. There are many situations where you will face a trade-off between the two and will have to decide which is more valuable to you.

One common situation is whether you want to call in an expert to do a repair or attempt it yourself. Knowing yourself and your skills helps here. For example, I've realized I'm terrible at plumbing. Let's say I need to replace an old, leaky faucet in my bathroom. I can pay a plumber $150 to do the job in an hour, or I can do it myself in four hours. If I don't have the $150 (or I want to spend the $150 on something else), I'll spend the four hours of my unskilled plumbing time on replacing the faucet. Here, I'm saving money but spending my labor.

Or, I can spend the $150 and have the plumber do the work and save my labor. Of course, even when hiring the plumber, my labor isn't zero. I've got to expend effort to find a reliable plumber (maybe by contacting friends for references), call and make the appointment, and be home while the plumber is doing the work.

People often face the labor-money trade-off at work. They might not know exactly how to do something, but an expensive consultant is available who knows the answer. In many organizations, there isn't the budget for a consultant. Or maybe the consultant is needed for an hour, but only works by the day or week. So, the employee spends many hours figuring out something a consultant could figure out in an hour. In the end, whether this is more cost-efficient for the company depends on how much time the employee spends figuring it out.

Another labor-money trade-off is grocery shopping. If you shop at a few stores, you'll notice different prices for similar (or the same) products. You can go to one store and get all your grocery items there, spending less labor shopping and more money. Or you can shop at two or more stores to get the lowest prices, spending more labor and less money. The landscape gets even more complicated when you take weekly store sale prices into account; maybe this week it's less expensive than usual to get soda at one store while they have a special sale.

Unfortunately, there isn't a universal answer to the labor-money trade-off. Each person decides what's best for them, given the amount of time (labor) and money they have. And for many of us, these things change with the ebb and flow of our life circumstances.

If someone has lots of money, they can save their labor by paying someone to do their dishes and laundry. I'm not there, so I did those chores myself. If you are just starting out, most likely you will too. But with any task, it's important to do the math, adding in the value of your time to the work equation before deciding your best course of action.

Now that we know what lean is, let's apply the concept to two labor-intensive chores and take a look at food management.

3

Lean Kitchen, Laundry, and Food Management

After learning to use resources efficiently at work, I applied the same principles to my bachelor household. I'd like to say my desire for a more attractive and efficient home motivated me, but it was my way of avoiding housework and reducing my labor.

A lot of labor is spent on housework. According to the Bureau of Labor Statistics, the average bachelor spends 1.07 hours per day on housework. This doesn't seem like much until you consider that amount of time adds up to over 390 hours per year. The average single woman spends 1.79 hours per day (over 653 hours per year) on housework. Guys, it's time to up our game!

To reduce as much housework as possible, I focused on

optimizing two labor-intensive chores—dishes and laundry.

This subject can be challenging to analyze because it involves values that vary among people. In my single household, I could easily determine my housekeeping standards on a day-to-day basis. Living alone and working long days, I valued cleanliness but not necessarily tidiness. When living with others, differences in the level of cleanliness and tidiness desired are common sources of conflict.

Using my values and lean principles, I developed the following optimized dishwashing and laundry processes.

Dishes

Before I jump into details of my process, keep in mind the primary aim of kitchen management is health and safety. Be sure dishes are clean and germ-free. Handle food according to safe handling and storage guidelines. There is plenty of information out there about these topics. Getting sick isn't any fun, so be diligent about the cleanliness of your kitchen and the freshness and safety of your food.

Before applying lean principles, the dish cycle looks like Version 1 (V1) below. This is our societal norm and illustrates how things "should" be done, according to most people who use a dishwasher.

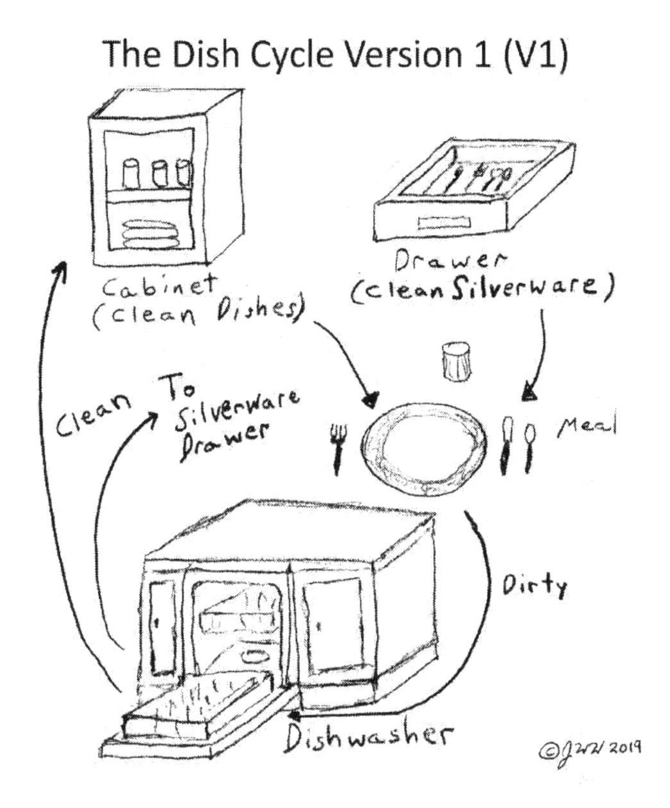

The process begins at the top of the diagram with clean dishes in the cabinet and clean silverware in the drawer. The dishwasher is empty. Before a meal, take the clean dishes from the cabinet and silverware from the drawer. After eating, rinse the dirty dishes and silverware and put them into the dishwasher. When the dishwasher is full (this may take up to a week for a single person), run the dishwasher. After the dishes are clean, put them away, and start the cycle again.

After living and examining this societal norm, I realized I could save labor, so I developed a lower effort Version 2 (V2) dish cycle.

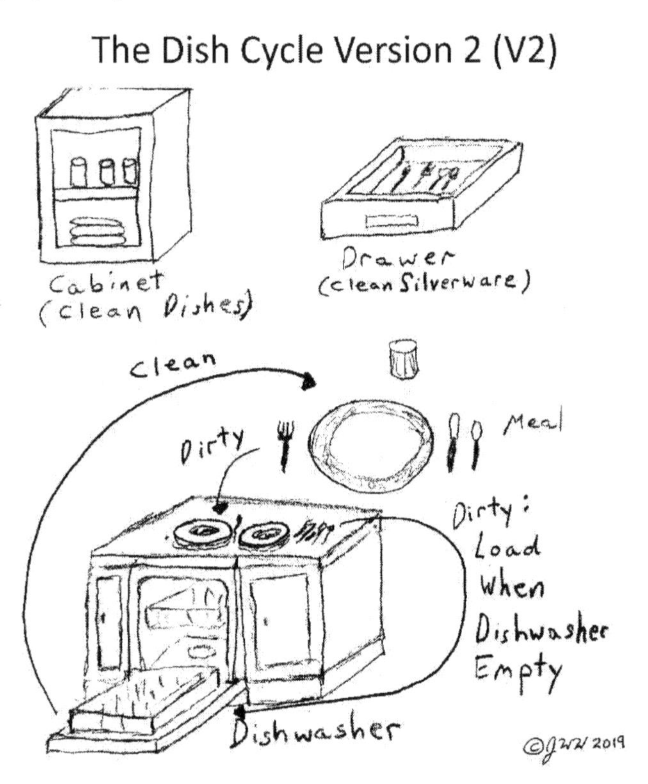

The Version 2 dish cycle starts with a clean load of dishes in the dishwasher and bypasses the cabinets and silverware drawer altogether. Before a meal, take the clean dishes and silverware out of the dishwasher and close the door. After eating, rinse the dishes and silverware and stack them neatly on the countertop. It's essential that the dishes and utensils are well rinsed, so they do not attract bugs. After several meals, when the dishwasher is empty or almost empty, load the dirty dishes from the countertop into the dishwasher. Run the dishwasher and start the cycle again with a dishwasher full of clean dishes. If you're good at managing this cycle, you won't need cabinets for dishes or a silverware drawer. You can repurpose this precious storage space to hold other household essentials.

A primary benefit of Version 2 is it eliminates the much-despised step of putting the dishes away. You take dishes out of the dishwasher as you need them, thus only unloading the dishwasher as dishes are needed, saving time and labor.

However, there is still an unnecessary step in Version 2. Before running the dishwasher, all the dirty dishes on top of the counter need to be loaded into the dishwasher. This inspired my creation of Version 3 (V3) of the dish cycle.

Version 3 (V3) is the most labor efficient, eliminating the most steps. In the lower right of the V3 drawing, you'll find a top view of the dishwasher rack, illustrating the dish rack and silverware holder are split between dirty and clean.

Version 3 starts with a dishwasher full of clean dishes. When preparing to eat a meal, take dishes and silverware from one side of the dishwasher rack and silverware holder.

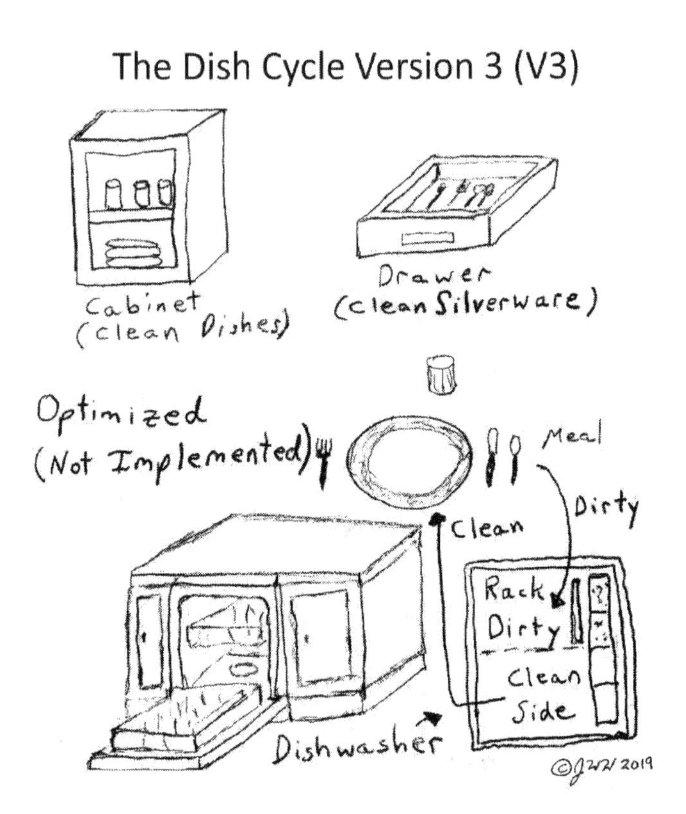

When the meal is over, replace the dishes back in the dishwasher where you took them out—setting up a dirty side of the dishwasher. As the week progresses, the dirty area of the dishwasher gradually grows, and the clean area gradually shrinks. When there are no more clean dishes left in the dishwasher, run the dishwasher, and begin the cycle again.

Version 3 is very labor efficient and has the added

benefit of not having dirty dishes piling up on your counter between loads. I experimented with Version 3 for a short period with two added conditions. Empty space existed between the clean dishes and the dirty dishes, and the dishwasher remained open, so dirty and clean dishes wouldn't live together in an enclosed, humid space. Remember, the cleanliness of your dishes is a primary factor in a healthy kitchen environment.

After hitting my shins on the open dishwasher door several times and being grossed out by having dirty and clean dishes close to each other, I stopped experimentation on Version 3 due to health and safety concerns. Nevertheless, Version 3 beautifully demonstrates a resource-efficient, lean concept. It also shows that lean resource concepts can be taken too far.

Let's look at the different dishwashing cycles described and map them on a Lean Dimensions figure comparing the different dishwashing cycles. The "X" next to each dishwashing cycle shows my rating of that cycle.

As a reminder, V1 is society's norm of how dishes are done. The dishes are put away after every run of the dishwasher. V2 saves work by leaving clean dishes in the dishwasher, using them as needed, and piling dirty dishes on top of the countertop until it's time to run the dishwasher again. V3 optimizes V2 by starting out with a dishwasher full of clean dishes, then replacing clean dishes with dirty dishes as the dishes are used.

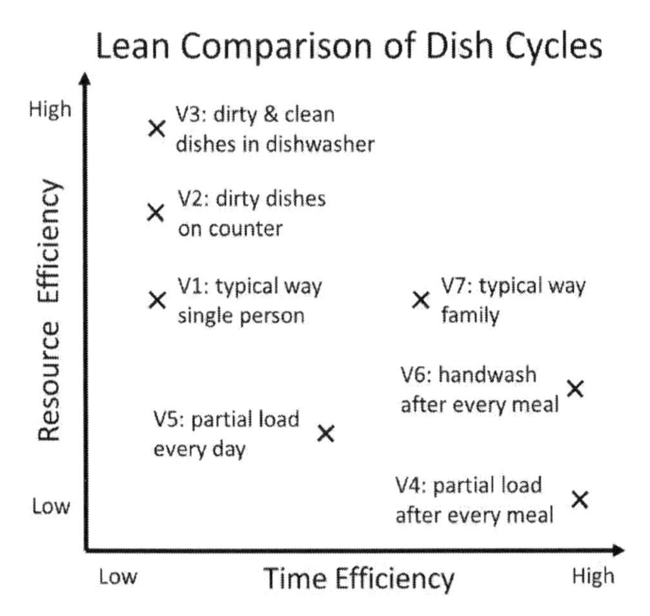

Moving from V1 to V3 achieves better resource efficiency, but all score low on time efficiency because dishes are done about every seven days (the time it took me as a single person to fill the dishwasher with dirty dishes).

Knowledge of lean theory illuminates more possibilities, as shown in the Lean Comparison figure. One is to run the dishwasher with only a few dishes after every meal (V4) or at the end of the day (V5). Dishes spend less time dirty, increasing time efficiency. However, V4 and V5 waste a lot of water and electricity because the dishwasher isn't full.

Another possibility is washing the dishes by hand after every meal, leaving them in a drying rack for the next meal (V6 on the figure). From a resource perspective, this is a trade-off—a dishwasher isn't necessary, little water or soap is needed, and fewer dishes are involved. But it takes more human labor as a resource instead of letting the dishwasher do the work. I did dishes using this process for about a year with excellent results. As my job got busier and my labor for dishwashing wasn't as available, I started delegating the washing to the dishwasher and went back to experimenting.

Finally, for completeness, I've added a Version 7 (V7) on the dishwashing comparison diagram to illustrate the typical dishwashing process as completed by a family. This method scores high in both resource and time efficiency because a family fills up the dishwasher frequently.

How does a single person achieve both high resource and high time efficiency? It's tough because most appliances are sized for a family or household of more than one person. Smaller, resource-efficient models designed for single occupant homes might be an option.

It is more resource-efficient to run a full dishwasher, but I've learned from observing others that a full dishwasher means different things to different people.

Loading the dishwasher optimally means putting as many dishes as you can in the dishwasher in such a way that the spraying water will clean all the dishes. This is highly dependent on the shapes and sizes of dishes and the type of spray system in the dishwasher. It will take some experimentation with a particular set of dishes in a particular dishwasher to pack as many dishes in, while still achieving maximum cleaning.

When a dishwasher seems full, I often spend a few minutes moving dishes and glasses around. I'm always amazed at how many more dishes I can fit into the dishwasher. Of course, my labor also increases when I do this. As with many situations in life, doing redundant tasks quickly in a resource-efficient way is useful, but this takes practice.

You may ask, what about pots and pans? My dishwasher didn't clean pots and pans very well, and they take up lots of space as compared to dishes, thus reducing the efficiency of the dishwasher. I always washed pots and pans by hand. I'm a big believer in soaking pots and pans before washing them and have learned that even five minutes of soaking can make an enormous difference.

There are some advanced techniques you can use to clean pots and pans, reducing your cleaning efforts. When cooking, don't let the food burn. This may seem obvious, but not burning your food can take years of practice and observation while cooking. When I was in college, a roommate burned some unidentified food onto a nice ceramic pan I had added to the communal kitchen. Sadly, I couldn't salvage the pan.

Another advanced technique involves washing pots and pans in two steps. First, get them what I call "mechanically clean." Scrape off any food remnants and goop left on the pan. Then, wash the pan with hot water and soap, so it is chemically and biologically clean, rinse, and dry.

The subject of drying pots and pans leads to another choice. Should you let pots and pans dry on a rack or dry them with a towel? I chose the lower-effort method of letting them dry on the rack. Here, standing water is your enemy. When you leave a washed pan right-side-up in the drying rack, standing water can take a long time to evaporate. The longer water sits, the more time germs and bacteria have to grow in this cozy moist environment.

When using a drying rack, carefully stack all the pots, pans, lids, and utensils, so there isn't any standing water. Period. I've found one of the biggest challenges is to stack the lids for pots and pans. After washing, water often collects in the lips of these lids. The best technique is to let the lids dry with the top (handle side) facing up, thus allowing water to flow out of the lip. You may need to experiment with your stacking technique a little. If the items in your drying rack aren't completely dry within a few hours after washing, you may need to add the additional step of drying your pans thoroughly with a towel.

To reduce the number of pots and pans I used, I often made one-pan dinners. I know I'm not alone here, as evidenced by the number of one-pot cookbooks out there.

At some point, while eating by myself, I adopted another dish-saving idea—skip the plate. I realized using a plate was a wasted resource, and I started to eat most hot meals right out of the pan. This is another example of where values are important. If you value eating off a nice plate more than the resources and time to wash that plate, then go ahead—eat off that plate! I saved the effort.

By eliminating a dish or two from each meal, I often stretched the length of time between dishwasher runs to ten days. Think of the energy and water savings! It helps to have extra silverware and some plastic spoons from fast-food restaurants.

Food

Since I was never sure when I would be eating meals at home, I bought mostly dried, frozen, and canned food.

As you shop, look at food labels carefully for nutrition

content. Some processed foods have a surprising amount of vitamin content, while others have almost none. In general, frozen vegetables seem to retain lots of vitamin content compared to canned vegetables. Canned pumpkin is an exception with an amazing amount of vitamin A. There are huge benefits to buying frozen food and dry goods that won't spoil quickly. It clears space in your fridge for the important stuff—beer, cheese, and leftover Chinese food!

Experiment with inventory management of food and other essential items to find what works best for your lifestyle and tastes. I decided early on that I didn't want to run out to the convenience store at midnight for toilet paper, soap, milk, or other essential items. Not only are things expensive at the convenience store, but those trips also waste a lot of time. I estimate I've saved thousands of gallons of gasoline and hundreds of hours by avoiding unnecessary trips to convenience stores.

One of my favorite inventory strategies is one I call the "one back" system. For example, if I don't want to run out of deodorant, I always keep an extra one at the back of the shelf. I keep enough inventory to last between trips to my favorite grocery or big-box store. There is always another one (or a week to ten day's supply, depending on the item) at the back of the shelf.

A similar concept, called Kanban, rose out of Japanese

manufacturing. Toyota is credited with creating the concept. The idea of Kanban is to balance demand and supply in a manufacturing setting. An auto factory might find that it needs to keep one-hundred engines in stock to meet its production goals. This is enough engines to ensure the factory won't run out, but not so many that money is wasted on inventory and factory floor space. If the supply of one-hundred engines goes down to sixty, an order for forty more engines goes to the engine manufacturing plant. This will get the auto factory stock back to one-hundred engines.

You can manage your household inventory in the same way. Based on my consumption, I decided it was good to keep two cans of baked beans in stock. If I used one can, then one can of baked beans went on the grocery list. If I used a second can before going to the store, a second can went on the grocery list. The next time I went to the store, I bought two more cans of baked beans, and I was all stocked up.

There are reasons to keep more than a week's supply of something. One reason is a good deal on something that isn't perishable. Make sure you can use it before it goes bad. I still relish the time I bought eight big cans of pumpkin on sale right after Thanksgiving, enough for a couple of years of pumpkin pies. Pay close attention to the expiration date on canned goods and other food in your stock. It doesn't save to have food go bad no matter how much you like pumpkin pie!

If running out of something like mayonnaise isn't critical, and you can live without it for a few days, wait until you run out to put it on your shopping list.

Another category is food you're about to run out of, but you would rather always have on hand. Put those items on your shopping list too. An example for me is sugar.

Then, there are food items I occasionally buy, like cucumbers. I don't put these on my regular shopping list. I get them when I'm at the grocery store, and they look appealing.

I like to have at least five cans of Spaghetti-O's on hand.

You decide what you want to keep on the don't-want-to-run-out-of list, the okay-to-run-out-of list, and the occasional list. These can be changed throughout your life as your needs change, but having your inventory needs settled can free up your thinking for more important matters.

Over time, I've tried to keep too much information in my head. When going to the store without a list, I would often end up with a lot of stuff I didn't need, while forgetting the stuff I needed. Having a list clears my head of the easy stuff that can be written down. There are many paper and electronic list creation tools available. Find one that works for you.

When I was single (and before the proliferation of smartphone apps), I kept a shopping list on a folded-up piece of paper in my wallet. That way, I always had it with me, whether at home or during an impromptu stop at the store.

Laundry

When considering lean laundry management, we need to revisit personal values. My sense of professionalism and pride didn't allow me to go to work or on dates in dirty or wrinkled clothes. I also wanted to avoid dingy business shirts and the dreaded pink underwear that results from washing a new red sweatshirt with white clothes. After several years of experience, I developed the optimized-value laundry cycle that accomplishes all these goals.

With the optimized-value cycle, you sort dirty laundry into three categories, as illustrated below. Starting at the top of the diagram, the three categories are:

- Blue jeans and other dark colors
- Light colors (like business shirts and khakis)
- Whites

These are all washed in separate loads due to their colors and the water temperature used.

Optimized-Value Laundry Cycle

Wear Clothes
Dirty laundry
Only wash full loads
sort
Load 1: Jeans, colors
Load 2: Khakis, Business Shirts
Load 3: Whites
Wash (cold) and dry
Wash (cold) and dry
Wash (hot) and dry
Fold or hang up soon
Hang up immediately to prevent wrinkles
Laundry basket (clean)
Select clothes to wear
© JWW 2019

As you examine the optimized-value laundry cycle, you may notice the absence of putting away clothes in dresser drawers. As in the case of dish management, I decided putting away most laundry is unnecessary. The exception is hanging up business shirts and pants immediately, preferably in the closet, to keep them from wrinkling. If I'm pressed for time, hanging them anywhere that keeps wrinkles from forming will work—like doorknobs, tops of doors, or the backs of chairs in a pinch.

I realize that having unwrinkled clothes and white (non-pink) underwear is not a universally held value. It led me to create another option—the optimized low-effort laundry cycle. This is the most popular cycle among college students.

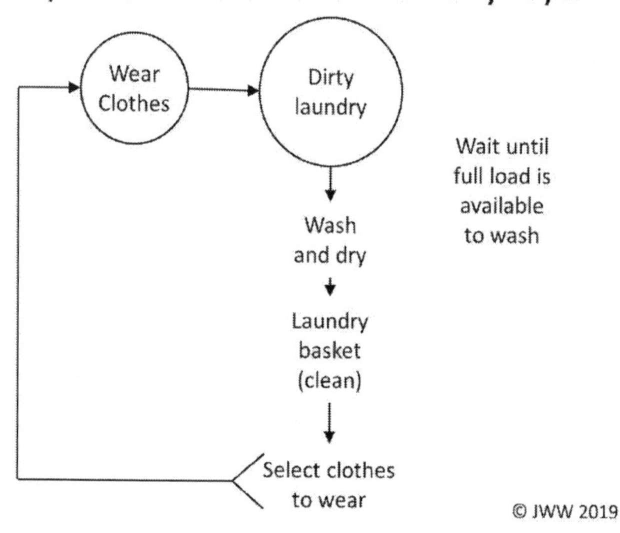

As can be seen in the figure, the optimized low-effort laundry cycle eliminates a lot of steps and the associated labor. This method allows for more frequent washing as there is no need to wait for an entire load of one type of laundry (colors, whites) to collect before washing. Your favorite clothing is washed as soon as there is a full load of dirty laundry. Full loads use resources (water, electricity, washer/dryer wear) efficiently. The laundry basket stores clean clothes, so no time is spent putting away clothes.

How do these laundry methods compare from a lean perspective? The Lean Comparison figure shows the two laundry methods.

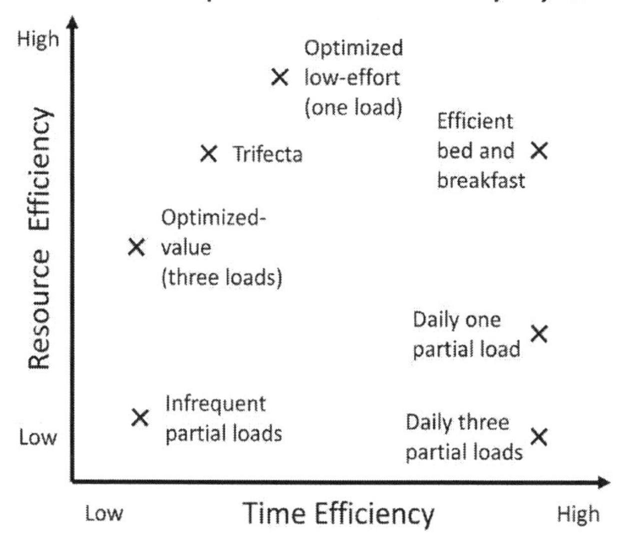

The optimized-value method uses resources efficiently, but the time efficiency is low because laundry is only done every seven to ten days.

The optimized low-effort method saves labor resources

(no sorting), and laundry is done more frequently, so it scores better on resource and time efficiency. But clothes are wrinkled, and over time, whites become grayer.

The figure can be used to evaluate other potential laundry cycles. Infrequent partial loads, a daily partial load, and three daily partial loads are mapped on the diagram. Most of us have done partial loads when we urgently needed a particular piece of clothing—this wastes a lot of resources.

When I lived in apartment buildings, the laundry rooms often had at least three washing machines and three dryers. When laundry day came, I would try to find a time when all three machines were empty. Unfortunately, this would usually be late in the evening. This allowed me to do all three loads of laundry simultaneously. I called this my laundry trifecta. From a labor efficiency perspective, it doesn't get any better.

What situation might lead to high resource and time efficiency for laundry? One possibility could be an efficient bed and breakfast. This efficient bed and breakfast creates enough laundry to do full loads every day of the different types of laundry. Resources are used efficiently, and the laundry gets done daily. The efficient bed and breakfast achieves both resource and time efficiency for laundry.

Further Laundry Optimization

In my years of doing laundry, I've learned many tips for laundry management. Some of the most useful tips involve the clothes I buy.

- Avoid buying anything other than underwear and weekend wear that isn't permanent press.

- Don't buy anything labeled "hand-wash" or "dry clean only."

- Have enough clothes in each of your color categories to last seven to ten days. This keeps you from doing laundry all the time and allows for full washer loads, saving energy and water.

- Buy socks in six or ten-pair packs, all the same color and design. This makes it easier to find a match when digging through the clean laundry basket. If you lose a sock (or get a hole in one), the remaining socks match several other socks.

- Except while washing clothes, moisture is your enemy. Allow any moist clothes, towels, or other dirty laundry to dry thoroughly before putting them in a hamper or dirty-clothes basket. Dry washed clothes as soon as possible, within twenty-four hours. Having mildew form on your clean or dirty laundry is disastrous.

- I'm a big fan of pretreating stains and smells in dirty laundry; this small effort results in much cleaner clothes.

I've tried modifications to my routine and have experimented to further optimize my laundry. I used to fasten the top button of my business shirts when hanging them on hangers to prevent them from falling off the hanger. After experimentation, I realized the unbuttoned shirts never fell off the hanger. So, I stopped this practice, undoubtedly saving hundreds of hours over my lifetime.

I once tried a "kitting" experiment. After doing laundry, I would "kit" or group together a clean pair of underwear, an undershirt, and a pair of dark socks—one kit for each day of the coming week. When getting ready in the morning, I grabbed an underwear kit and didn't have to fish through the clean laundry basket. Although I didn't keep exact records, the kitting seemed to take too much time, so I dropped the process after a couple of months.

The kitting experiment brings up another interesting point about time and task management. Even though a task may take more time to do in advance, doing so might save precious time later or reduce stress. Kitting together a pair of socks, underwear, and a t-shirt might save time in the morning when you are running late for work. Laying out your clothes the night before helps you relax and sleep well before early meetings or your commute.

Running these kinds of experiments is useful. Who knows? You might find solutions that make your life easier. Try your own variations to see what works best for you. If you're experimenting, keep data.

Fashion

When selecting clothes to wear for the day, I separate colors into two categories:

1. Colors that go with black
2. Colors that go with brown

When dressing in the morning, I decide on a black or brown theme for the day, then select color-coordinated clothes.

Colors that go with black are white, blue, gray, and red.

Colors that go with brown are white, green, and some blues.

I avoid yellow and orange except as an accent color. Khakis and jeans are popular because they go with almost any color shirt. A pair of black shoes and a black belt or a pair of brown shoes and a brown belt complete my outfit. I figured out these basics on my own without ever reading anything about fashion.

After getting married, my wife taught me other useful fashion rules like socks should match your pants, not your shoes. The exception is sneakers, which should always be worn with white socks. Never wear socks with sandals ever! Finally, don't wear denim shirts with denim jeans. I may have violated this last one a few times during my single days.

Lean kitchen and laundry practices saved me countless hours of housework and will save you time too. When devising any lean process, consider your values, goals, health impact, budget, and the time and effort it will take to get your desired result.

In the next chapter, we will look at situations that are more complicated and complex than dishes, laundry, and food management.

When making a lean change at work are you doing the equivalent of putting clean dishes next to dirty dishes—violating some quality objective?

4

Complicated and Complex Household Situations

If managing a household was as simple as doing the dishes and the laundry, then we could optimize these tasks to suit our needs. We could relax and manage our households with ease.

Unfortunately, household situations arise that we don't know how to handle, and experts need to be called in.

Even worse are household situations where even the experts don't know how to handle a problem. Some experts might claim to know what to do, but they experiment until they figure out a solution to a problem.

So, what do you do in these situations? How do you figure out what to do when outlier situations like these arise? It's useful to have a tool to assess these unusual situations.

A useful framework is the Cynefin (pronounced kuh-NEV-in) framework, which was developed by Dave Snowden. In the following explanation, I've drawn heavily on Snowden's work. In the references, more complete descriptions of the Cynefin framework are available.

Over the past few years, working in agile ways has been talked about and implemented in many industries—especially in high-tech product development. The Cynefin framework is the basis for these more agile ways of working. Applying this knowledge will allow you to run an agile household too.

First, let's classify problems from a complexity standpoint. There are four different kinds of situations or problems you might face in a household. The four types of problems are:

- Obvious
- Complicated
- Complex
- Chaotic

These situation classifications are easily described using a figure of the Cynefin framework.

The Cynefin figure is separated into five different areas, one for each type of household problem and one to address the unknown. This unknown area is between the other areas and is called disorder. Looking at a problem, using this framework, will help you make sense out of situations so you can confidently come up with how to approach a problem.

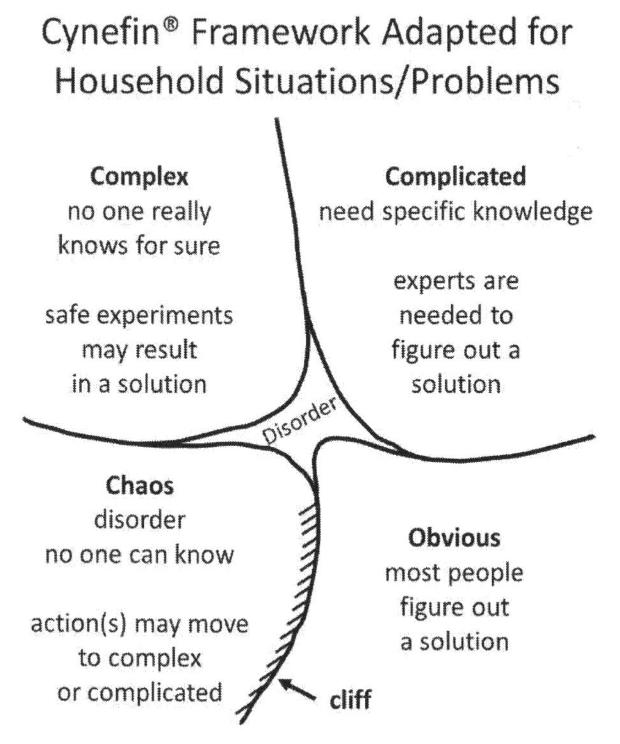

Obvious Problems

In the lower right of the figure are obvious situations. In obvious situations, most people know or can figure out household processes and solutions that meet their needs. Examples of these situations are doing the dishes and laundry. Although I've presented my bachelor-optimized ways of doing these chores, most people have some process of getting these tasks done, and they get along fine—whether their processes are optimized or not.

A key thing about obvious situations and problems is that optimum solutions are possible that meet the desired outcome and quality standard. In doing my laundry, my quality standards were clean, unwrinkled business shirts and khakis and whites that weren't dingy. For obvious problems, best practices can be developed.

Complicated Problems

In the upper right of the figure are complicated household situations. These are situations most people don't know how to handle and that require expert, specific knowledge. Expertise is not only knowledge but also skills and tools to do a job.

As an alternative to using experts, a person can research

and learn about the situation. After learning more, they can take care of the situation on their own—or they may still call an expert if they determine they cannot handle the problem on their own. As an example, the roof of my ranch house started leaking. Looking at the twenty-year-old shingles, I realized I had to replace the roof. Even though I knew what needed to be done, I couldn't do the work myself. I obtained a few quotes on the job. One roofing company suggested adding special materials to parts of the roof to prevent future leaks. I picked that company; there was no way I had the knowledge, skills, or tools to do the job myself.

Another interesting characteristic of complicated problems is that different experts may come up with different but adequate solutions. Let's say someone decides to add a 200 square foot addition onto their home. They contact two different architects who supply design ideas. You can guarantee the architects will come up with different plans. Here, you can only hold the architects to good practices for their plans. In this case, good practices would be that the plans follow local building codes and call for adequate construction practices.

Complex Problems

There are some problems that even experts don't know with certainty how to resolve. These complex situations are represented in the upper left of the diagram.

Steps can be taken that might solve a complex problem, but the outcome isn't predictable. Here, safe-to-fail experiments can be done to see if the desired result is obtained. A safe-to-fail experiment is a limited, small-scale experiment that won't result in harm or loss. Either an expert can try the experiment, or the homeowner can. If the experiment solves the problem, that's wonderful! If the problem isn't solved, then another safe-to-fail experiment is tried. People usually don't like to hear their home is being experimented on. You know you're dealing with a complex situation when a household repair expert says something like, "Well, we can try this to fix the problem, but we can't guarantee the result."

I have a friend who lived in a house with wooden cedar shingles and dormer windows that resulted in a complex roof configuration. There was a leak around one of the dormer windows, but the cedar shingles appeared to be in good shape. His roofing expert said they would try to fix the leak, but the result wasn't certain. It took the roofing company three tries (experiments) throughout several rainstorms to completely fix the leak. He had a complex problem on his hands.

In a business setting, agile product development sits on the boundary between complex and complicated. This is where experts have an idea of what to do, but they're not completely sure, so safe-to-fail experiments are needed.

Chaos

The lower left of the diagram is chaos. This is an area of unpredictability—there are no patterns to what's going on. When facing a chaotic problem, taking action to bring the problem into the complex domain is all that can be done. Once in the complex domain, a potential resolution to the problem can be found using safe-to-fail experiments.

There can be a danger to becoming complacent about obvious problems and situations. If enough attention isn't paid to obvious problems, they may fall over a cliff into chaos. This can also happen if complex or complicated problems are misclassified as obvious problems. We'll talk more about this in chapter eight.

Disorder

Finally, there is a fifth area in the middle of the figure labeled

"Disorder." This is when you don't know what area your problem is in and; therefore, it's difficult to know what problem-solving method to apply. If someone is facing a problem like this, one solution is to break the problem down into different parts. Then, each part of the problem can be examined and handled appropriately depending on whether the part is obvious, complicated, complex, or chaotic.

The Cynefin framework is a handy guide on how to approach different types of situations and problems—whether at home or at work. In the next chapter, we'll look at a few of the unusual problems I faced in my household to give you real-world examples you might find handy when dealing with your own household issues.

5

Dealing with Unusual Challenges

During my time as a bachelor, I dealt with several types of unusual problems. See if you can make sense of the problem using the Cynefin framework. I'll share my viewpoint at the end of the chapter.

The Revenge of Oil

An unusual feature of my 1950s ranch house was an oil tank of unknown capacity. This oil tank lived in the basement, half-hidden under the stairway. Painted battleship gray, it didn't match anything else in the basement, certainly not the orange concrete wall behind it or the green, speckled tile beneath it.

The tank hovered a foot off the floor on legs made of

steel pipes. It had rounded edges on the top and bottom and was about four feet high by two feet wide by six feet long. The tank was much too big to take up the stairs and out of the house and must have been installed when the house was built.

When I moved in, there was a natural gas furnace in the house. In the Chicago area, most people stopped using oil-burning furnaces decades ago. When I had the house inspected before buying it, the inspector vaguely pointed at the oil tank and gave it a few good thumps on the side. The hollow noise that resulted sounded like the Tin Man before he got his heart in *The Wizard of Oz,* indicating the tank was empty.

After this extensive evaluation, the inspector pointed at the tank, shrugged his shoulders, and said, "I guess it's not hurting anything."

Note to home buyers—if you run across this situation, insist any unused oil tank(s) or other old, out-of-date, and not functional equipment is removed before you buy the house.

As a first-time home buyer, concerned about other things, and lacking this knowledge, I nodded my head in agreement with the inspector and forgot about the oil tank.

For well over a decade after I moved in, the tank stood benignly in the basement next to the washing machine and dryer.

Given my work schedule and optimized infrequency of doing laundry, there were times I didn't go into the basement for several days. One day, as I headed down the stairs, an acrid petroleum smell pierced my nostrils. I looked around for a leaking paint or turpentine can. Nothing. The next day, I went into the basement again, and sure enough, there was that smell again. I searched around and discovered the oil tank was leaking.

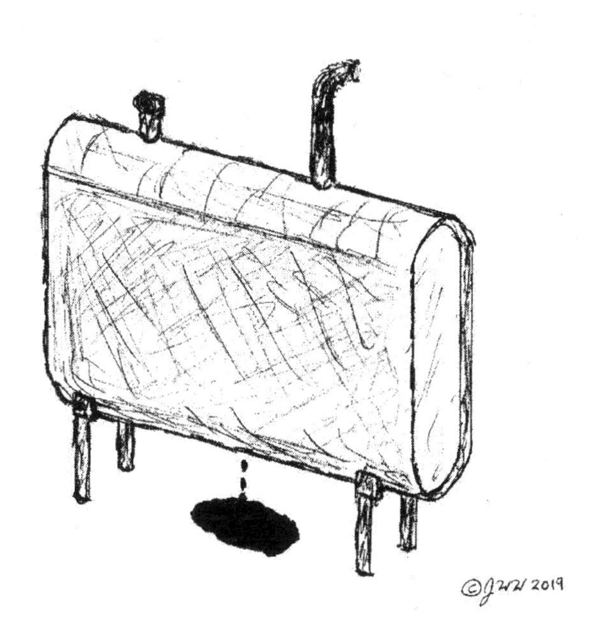

Drip, drip, drip. Slowly, the oil was leaking out of the bottom of the tank, forming a slick, pungent puddle on the floor.

After a quick internet search, I learned one way to clean up small oil spills is to use kitty litter. I made a late-night run to the store, and an hour later, I had a cardboard box lined with a plastic garbage bag filled with kitty litter. I placed my creation under the oil tank, hoping the leak would be over in a day or two. The next day, when I came home from work, I checked the situation. Oil was still dripping, and the kitty litter was saturated. I changed the kitty litter to absorb more of the oil.

The old oil tank kept leaking for over a week, triggering my I've-got-to-do-something-else threshold. Internet searches suggested things could be worse. Some homeowners faced old, abandoned oil tanks buried in their yards, creating an even more complex environmental disaster by leaking oil into the ground. Whew! I'd escaped that problem. But I still had no idea what to do about my problem.

To get a better sense of what I was dealing with, I tried to figure out how much oil was still in the tank. I created a kind of dip stick out of two three-foot-long wooden dowels. I carefully duct-taped the ends of the dowels together so the dipstick could reach the bottom of the tank, took the cap off the filler pipe on the top of the tank, and inserted my makeshift measuring stick.

That's when I learned that wood makes a poor dipstick.

Oil soaked into the wood, so the oil level in the tank wasn't apparent. However, my attempted measurement gave me a vague idea that there were still many gallons of oil left in the tank. How long would it take for that much oil to drip out? I had no clue.

I decided the oil tank had to go. After several phone calls, I found a place that would cut up and remove the tank, but the tank had to be empty before they would perform their service. I kept looking.

During my internet searches, I learned that home heating oil is like diesel fuel and classified as hazardous waste. After many more phone calls, I found a properly certified company that would pump out the oil and dispose of it properly. At this point, I also had two boxes of kitty litter soaked with hazardous oil to get rid of.

I made all the necessary arrangements to empty and remove the tank and haul the whole mess away.

A few days later, a guy arrived with a big tank truck along with a pump and hoses long enough to reach the tank in the basement. He pumped out the remaining heating oil.

The next day, three other guys arrived to cut the oil tank into pieces small enough to carry up the basement stairs and out of the house. They used a power saw with a six-inch reciprocating blade capable of cutting steel. Fortunately, the tank was empty, so they didn't blow themselves or my house up, for which I am thankful. They neatly piled the tank pieces and bags of kitty litter on a trailer behind their truck and whisked it all away for proper disposal.

I spent a couple hours cleaning up the basement floor where the tank had been, using an environmentally friendly cleaner to attack the oily mess. Despite my best efforts, that area of the basement floor was never quite the same.

My personal oil spill was over. Finally.

Small Animals Want to Live with Me

The suburbs are often filled with wildlife, especially smaller animals such as birds, chipmunks, and squirrels. Before becoming a homeowner, I enjoyed watching chipmunks collect food in their puffy cheeks and squirrels romp through the grass looking for nuts.

Now that I own a home and live in an area that can get brutally cold in the winter, I've realized that these same animals want to share my warm, dry home. And when those cute animals come inside, it's not so pleasant.

Once animals enter what architects call the "building envelope," it can be challenging to decide what to do. I wondered if I should seek professional help. Because I didn't want to hurt these cute animals, I was left in a quandary about what to do when they got into my house.

Birds I

Birds pose problems because they can fly anywhere.

The painted cedar siding on my house peeled easily. In the winter, moisture from inside the house drove through the wood siding and pushed the paint off the boards. Back in the 1950s, they didn't have vapor barriers to control this moisture. To prevent moisture from pushing the paint off the house, an earlier owner installed many two-inch round metal vents in the outside siding at the top and bottom of the walls.

While watching a *MASH* rerun on TV one spring day, I heard a pecking noise on the siding. When I popped out the door, a bird flew quickly away. I surmised a woodpecker had decided the edge of a siding vent would be a good place to peck. Thinking that was the end of it, I resumed watching TV.

A couple of days later, I arrived home and spotted a two-inch diameter hole in the siding next to one of the vents. The hole was big enough for a woodpecker to move in and make a home between the siding and the inside wall of my house. Uggghhh!

I confirmed the existence of birds when I heard fluttering sounds inside the wall as I watched TV that evening.

I could have patched the hole, but that meant possibly trapping birds inside the wall. That would not only kill the birds but would also leave me with an awful smell as the birds decomposed and no easy or pleasant way to remove them.

What to do?

I decided to wait and see. I couldn't wait too long because I didn't want woodpeckers raising a family in my wall. If baby birds hatched, I would be living with them for some time.

Fortunately, I got lucky. The following Saturday, I arrived home from running errands and saw two adult birds fly out of the hole. I stuffed a rag in the hole, blocking the access. Listening, I didn't hear any fluttering inside the wall. Over the next few hours, I filled the hole with layers of wood putty. I put more coats on in subsequent days, which was enough to keep the birds away. No more woodpeckers in the wall.

Birds II

Another bird invasion happened after I painted the soffits on the house. To paint the soffits, I removed the rectangular soffit vents. When I finished painting late one evening, it was too dark to nail the vents back in place. Instead, as a temporary measure, I placed the rectangular vents inside the holes in the plywood soffit without nailing them. At the time, this was a perfectly acceptable shortcut since gravity held the vent in place inside the rectangular hole.

As the days went by, and I was busy with other chores and work, my temporary fix became not so temporary. I didn't get around to nailing the vents back on the soffits.

One day, a few months later, I walked by that area of the house and noticed something had moved the vent aside, leaving an opening into the attic.

The Vent Pushed Aside

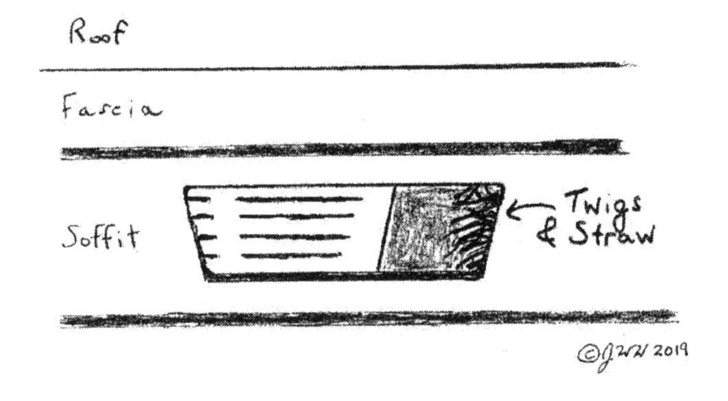

How the heck would a bird, a bat, or some other animal know enough to go to the vent, push up on it, and then nudge it aside? This is still a mystery to me.

Upon further examination, and much to my dismay, I noticed that whatever creature had done this had piled twigs and straw inside on the attic side of the plywood soffit. The critter was making itself a cozy home.

This situation posed an even greater quandary than the woodpecker hole. The bird (I assumed it was a bird) could be anywhere in my cavernous attic.

Using the end of a broomstick, I repositioned the soffit vent, so it completely covered the hole again. I left the vent unattached so the creature could escape. The next day, I came home from work and, sure enough, the vent had moved again. I repositioned the vent to cover the hole again. After doing this for several days in a row, the critter either got frustrated and left or died in some remote corner of the attic. The vent didn't move anymore for several days. I never smelled anything decaying inside the house, so the creature must have moved out. This time, I nailed the vent to the soffit as I should have in the first place. I never saw the beast(s) I was up against.

Squirrel I

One autumn day, I came home from work especially late. It was dark. Soon after arriving, I noticed telltale signs that something was amiss. A stuffed-animal bunny that usually sat on the fireplace mantel was on the floor. There was a small pile of fresh wood chips under the couch, apparently chewed off the couch frame. I searched room by room for other signs of disturbance. In the bathroom, I noticed familiar-looking, small, ashen paw prints in the bathtub. Then, I knew for sure—squirrel!

I went back to the fireplace and looked at the damper. It was open. I usually kept it closed when I wasn't burning logs in the fireplace. I guessed a squirrel had fallen down the chimney, and the force had opened the damper. Voila, the squirrel was in! Once inside the fireplace, he had scurried through the fireplace screen and into my house. I imagine, to the squirrel, being inside the house must have felt like the Wonderland Alice found after falling down a rabbit hole.

Attributing much more intelligence to the squirrel than it probably deserved, I guessed that once inside, the squirrel knew the way out must be up. It probably climbed up the mantel, saw the stuffed bunny, and thought he'd found a new friend. Dismayed to realize the bunny wasn't real, the squirrel had thrown the rabbit to the floor. Realizing that going up did not lead to freedom, the squirrel chewed on the couch frame a bit before visiting the bathtub and who knows where else. Luckily, the packaged food on the kitchen counters was untouched.

I looked around the house. Where was the critter? With 1,400 square feet on the first floor and 1,000 square feet of basement, there were many nooks, crannies, closets, and boxes where the squirrel could hide. Where could the squirrel be? I listened carefully. Silence. I assumed the squirrel was hiding from me somewhere, frozen in fear.

I wondered what I would do if I found the furry little intruder; what would I do when I found myself face-to-face with him? I didn't have a good answer.

I thought about getting professional help. Was there a business that specialized in home squirrel removal? I imagined calling such a company and how the conversation might go.

"Hello, this is Ajax Animal Removal. How can I help you?"

"Hello, do you remove squirrels from houses?"

"Yes, we do! How can we help?"

"I think there's a squirrel in my house. My fireplace damper is open, there are chewed wood shavings under the couch, and paw prints in the bathtub. I recognize them as squirrel paw prints." I decided to leave out the part about the stuffed bunny.

"Where is the squirrel now?"

"I don't know, I haven't actually seen it."

"Is it possible the squirrel left the house?"

"I don't think so. I don't know how it would have gotten out."

"Unfortunately, all of our squirrel finders have gone

home for the evening. If you want, I can have someone call you back in the morning."

"What should I do tonight?"

"Watch a movie with small animals in it. This usually draws them out. *Caddy Shack* is a good one. That gopher is hilarious. *Christmas Vacation* is another classic with an actual squirrel hiding in the Christmas tree! I'm just kidding. The squirrel will hide from you."

"Okay, thanks. Goodnight."

"Goodnight and good luck!"

I decided not to call anyone. I went into do-it-yourself mode and headed to my local Home Depot. Was there such a thing as a squirrel trap?

One advantage of our capitalist system is that many of our needs are anticipated before we even know we have them. It turned out Home Depot sold a trap that would catch the squirrel alive. Just what I needed! I bought the trap and headed for home.

The trap was a long and narrow cage constructed out of metal bars about the width of a pencil lead. It was just big enough to hold an adult squirrel. There was a trapdoor at one end of the cage. Food could be placed on a tray at the opposite end. The squirrel was supposed to enter the cage through the trapdoor and head to the other end to get the food. Eating the food on the tray would trip a mechanism that would shut the trapdoor, capturing the squirrel.

I set the trap up on the kitchen floor with plenty of newspapers underneath, figuring the squirrel would be in distress when captured. The kitchen had the most easily cleanable floor and was next to the room with the fireplace. Most importantly, the kitchen was at the opposite end of the house from my bedroom. I didn't want to be close to the action.

I put some tasty peanut butter on the food tray inside the trap. What more could a squirrel want?

I decided against trying to find the squirrel before going to bed, but I wanted to prevent the little guy from attacking me while I was sleeping. I didn't need to wrestle a squirrel. I searched my bedroom and closet thoroughly and found no signs of the squirrel in the bedroom. I shut the bedroom door and tried to go to sleep.

After a restless night spent without hearing a trap mechanism spring or any other commotion, I went to the kitchen.

Staring at me with black, glassy eyes through the square openings in the metal cage was a live squirrel.

What to do now?

The most obvious place to take the squirrel was a park about a quarter of a mile away. This was close enough to walk and probably far enough away that the little creature wouldn't find his way back to bother me again.

Thinking my plan through, I wondered what could happen on the way to the park. I imagined carrying the trap with a live, agitated squirrel inside. If someone was walking their dog, chaos might ensue. Not pretty. The trap had a little handle on it, with the operative word being little. The handle was only an inch or two away from the cage.

My mind raced. I wasn't comfortable holding onto the small handle with my hand so close to the ferocious teeth and razor-sharp claws of a potentially rabid rodent.

To solve this problem, I used long pliers to grab the handle and lift the squirrel-filled cage into a big, plastic storage bin. After putting the lid on the bin, I walked to the park carrying the container, pliers, and a broom.

I arrived without incident, and I didn't run across anyone walking their dog, nosy neighbors wondering what I was doing, or people too puzzled or afraid to ask. When I got to the park, I used the pliers to pull the trap out of the storage bin.

Fortunately, the trap came with release instructions. The flick of a lever would release the trapdoor, and the squirrel could escape. The lever also seemed to be within biting range of the squirrel. How close did I want to be from the released squirrel? Not close at all. This is where the broom came in handy.

Using the broom handle to maintain distance from the trap, I flicked the release lever. Whoever wrote the trap instructions must have been naive or had a sense of humor. The instructions said once the lever was released, the trapdoor would open, and the squirrel would walk away. In my case, once I opened the door, the squirrel ran away faster than any squirrel I've ever seen! The escaping squirrel is only a blur in my memory.

Walking home, satisfied, I made a note in my mental household to-do list to put chicken wire on top of the fireplace chimney so no more squirrels, birds, or other animals could get in.

Back at home, I dealt with the mess the squirrel had made of my place. Little surprises were here and there on the carpeting and on the top of the couch. I spent the better part of the weekend thoroughly cleaning upholstery and carpeting.

Since it was fall, and the days were becoming colder and shorter, I had to put off getting on the roof to install the chicken wire on the chimney. I didn't get to it before the snow started flying. As a half measure, I propped a board underneath the fireplace damper handle. If the same thing happened again, at least the squirrel wouldn't get loose in the house.

The winter went by uneventfully, at least on the squirrel

front.

Squirrel II

One Sunday, early the next spring, I awoke to new sounds, so strange they are hard to describe. There were scratching, thumping, and moving sounds like something trapped inside a tin can. I followed the sounds to the fireplace at the opposite end of the house.

Something was stuck in the metal chimney.

The board I had placed under the damper handle was still firmly in place. Whatever was in there was stuck. Who would have thought my fireplace would be such an effective trap?

Now what?

Luckily, it was a Sunday. I had time to think. Given the sounds and lack of chirping, I was sure I was dealing with another squirrel or a small mammal. I considered the following options:

- Option 1: Leave the squirrel in the chimney. The unfortunate squirrel would die slowly and painfully. How long would that take? How would I know when it was dead? I'd still have to remove the dead squirrel. Not pleasant for the squirrel or me.

- Option 2: Open the fireplace damper and let him out. While maintaining distance from the fireplace, I could use a piece of rope to open the damper. What if the squirrel bolted out of the fireplace and ran into the house? If I left a door open, he might find the door and run outside. Or would the rodent run and hide in the house? If the squirrel was loose in the house, I could catch it with my handy, new squirrel trap, just like I had caught the first one. In the meantime, I would be left with the mess the squirrel would make and an unsettling night of sleep. The potential of squirrel poop in the house again didn't make this choice attractive.

After pondering these options, I went back to the drawing board and several more hours of thinking.

As evening approached, I finally thought of an acceptable solution that required some construction. My design involved taking a piece of plywood big enough to cover the fireplace opening and cutting a rectangular hole in it. The rectangular hole would be the same size as the end of the squirrel trap. I'd drill a second, smaller, round hole in the plywood for the fireplace poker, which I would use to knock down the board holding the damper shut and to open the damper. The plywood would hold the squirrel in the fireplace. Hopefully, the squirrel would eventually run through the hole in the plywood directly into the trap I'd place in front of my contraption.

I found a piece of old paneling and moved the squirrel trap and necessary tools into the garage to begin construction.

Situations like these are where having tools on hand, and spare parts around the house pays off.

Within an hour, I finished my masterpiece. I placed my carefully crafted piece of plywood against the fireplace and aligned the trapdoor-end of the squirrel trap with the custom rectangular hole. To further entice the squirrel, I put peanut butter on the bait tray. To keep everything in place, I positioned random barbell weights around the trap and against the paneling. Finally, I put the poker through the hole at the top of the paneling.

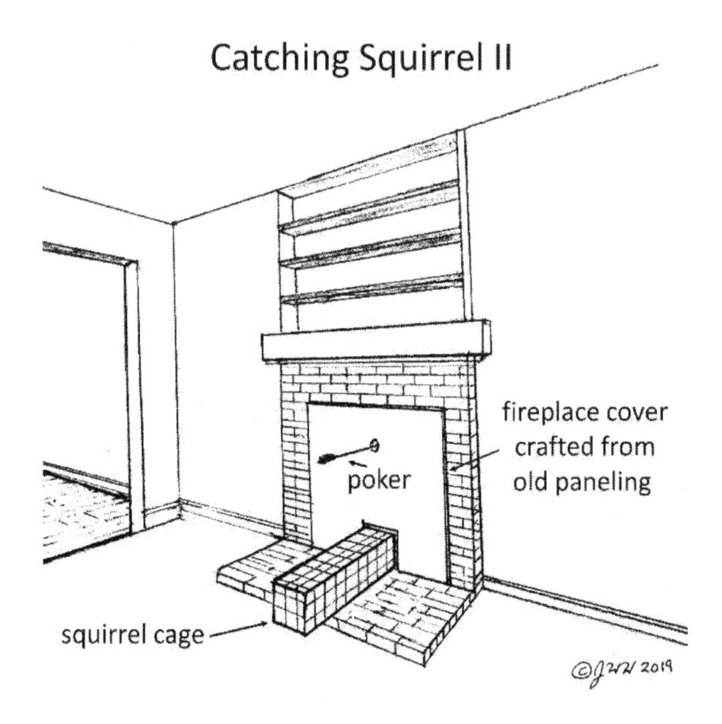

Now that paneling covered the fireplace opening, I couldn't see the damper handle or the board that held the damper handle shut. I fished around with the poker and knocked down the board, but the damper remained closed. Then, I fished around to find the damper handle, hooked it with the end of the poker, and tried to open the damper. No luck.

The poker was at a strange angle to the damper handle, and I couldn't get enough downward force on the handle to open it. After several attempts, I took a break. It had been a long day of thinking and improvising, and I was getting hungry.

While in the kitchen foraging for some food, I heard a commotion and the sound of the trapdoor snapping shut. Back at the fireplace, in the cage, was Squirrel II!

I knew what to do from here. Grabbing the big bin, pliers, and broom, I took Squirrel II to the park and released it.

I was quite proud of my squirrel catching device. It was a splendid example of what I call use-what-you-have design, saving a trip to a home improvement store or a potentially expensive visit from a rodent catcher. I was glad I had kept the trap from the first squirrel.

Putting chicken wire at the top of the chimney moved to the top of my to-do list, and I made that modest improvement quickly. No more squirrel incidents occurred for the rest of the time I lived in that house.

Before I moved and married, several years later, I held a garage sale to get rid of all the stuff I no longer needed. Sadly, the squirrel trap didn't make the "essential things to move" list. I put it up for sale at the bargain price of $5, which seemed reasonable for an item that cost $20 to $30 new. A guy at the garage sale showed interest in the trap but had to make a phone call first. He walked away, so I'm not sure who he called or what he asked. Maybe he called his broker to check the market price of used squirrel traps. After the call ended, he came back and offered me $3. Sold!

Stories in the Context of the Cynefin Framework

Have you been thinking about these situations with respect to the Cynefin framework?

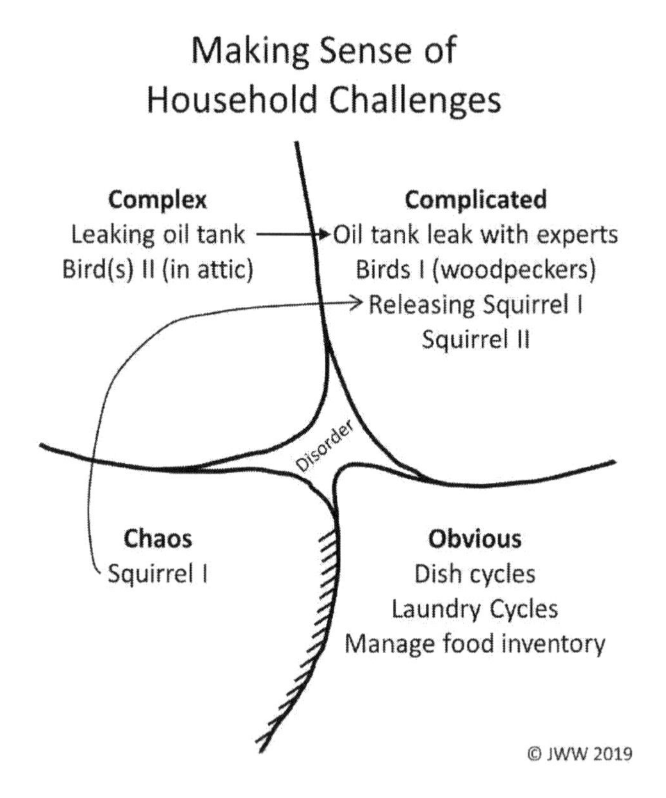

The figure above shows where I've placed the cycles from earlier in the book and challenges from this chapter on the Cynefin framework.

In the obvious area are the dish and laundry cycles and managing food inventory. One doesn't have to be an expert to do these tasks.

The Birds I (woodpeckers) and catching Squirrel II are complicated situations that could be resolved satisfactorily in several different ways. Experimentation wasn't needed; thinking about how to approach each of these situations and persistence solved the problems.

Experimentation was needed to deal with the birds (or other beasts) in the attic, so this situation ended up in the complex area. I wasn't sure what would resolve the problem, so I experimented safely.

The leaking oil tank problem started out as complex. I didn't know what to do, so I started out trying to collect the leaking oil in a box filled with kitty litter. That experiment didn't work, so I did more research on the internet. Finally, experts were called in. The problem then moved into the complicated area. When I engaged the right experts, the solution became apparent—the oil tank had to be drained and removed.

This emphasizes that even though work is obvious, this doesn't mean anyone can do it without the right skills and equipment. In the case of the oil tank, two types of expertise were needed. One company drained the tank, another removed it.

The Squirrel I problem started in the chaotic domain. Why? In the case of Squirrel I, I didn't know what was going on, so I had to act by setting the squirrel trap. I had not seen the squirrel, only its footprints. I also acted by searching my bedroom for the critter before I went to bed. Catching this first squirrel stabilized the situation. I had the trap instructions on how to release the squirrel. I thought through the release and added my own steps so I wouldn't get bitten. Once the first squirrel was captured, what remained was a complicated problem.

After catching the first squirrel, I had knowledge of the squirrel trap and how to let a live squirrel loose. My knowledge made it easier to catch and release the second squirrel. Dealing with Squirrel II was a complicated design problem resolved by building the custom plywood fireplace enclosure.

Whew! Now that we've mastered the theory and practice of handling challenging household situations, it's time for some lighter material. Let's visit home decorating.

When facing an unusual challenge at work ask yourself if you are dealing with a Squirrel I type of problem (never seen before) or a Squirrel II type of problem (like something seen before but with differences). A little thought in advance goes a long way to saving you time and effort in the long run.

6

Decorating

There may be theories behind decorating a home, but I don't know what they are. If you're moving into your first place, likely, you don't either. The following descriptions may seem a bit minimalist, but minimalism can save a lot of stuff, and thus save the environment too. Start here when deciding how to decorate your home. You can always expand your horizons later.

Froufrou

Many bachelor pads distinctly lack froufrou and feminine touches. It's not that men don't appreciate these things; most of us simply haven't taken the time, effort, and expense to deploy them in our caves. Many women also prefer a less cluttered, minimalist style.

When I visit friends, I notice touches like candles, vases with flowers, plants, and even matching towels and linens in the kitchen or bathroom. When I see these items, I think, "Wow, that's a nice touch!" But then, I usually do not adopt any of it. Some froufrou items you would never have found in my bachelor home are:

- Facial tissues or tissue holders. I used toilet paper to blow my nose.

- Houseplants that need watering more than once a month. Small ficus trees are great houseplants because if you forget to water them, just a few leaves start turning brown and dropping before the whole plant dies. Once you notice a few leaves turning yellow and dropping, water the ficus tree thoroughly. It will perk right up and stop losing leaves.

- Flower or greenery arrangements made of silk or satin.

- Valences over the tops of mini blinds.

- More than one pillow per person on beds. Decorative pillows on top of the bed are especially froufrou.

- More than two pillows on a couch or one on a chair.

- A fabric shower curtain or one with an inner liner and an outer decorative shower curtain.

After several years, one froufrou thing I did adopt was a bed ruffle. Not because they looked nice, but because they hid the junk I stuffed under the bed.

Formal Dining

Despite what I described above, occasionally, I wanted to impress guests like my parents or a special someone by having them over for a meal. I didn't want them to think I was totally uncivilized. For these occasions, I had matching plates and flatware that had a heavy feel to it.

If you really want to impress guests, use cloth napkins and nice glasses. Focus on presentation and atmosphere to make the meal a memorable experience.

Efficiency can go out of the window when presenting a nice meal.

Use your best manners for these occasions. A little effort makes a big impression.

I learned to cook a few different meals that I like, had some universal appeal, and were relatively easy to make. Three of my go-to meals are stew made in a crockpot, spaghetti with marinara sauce (meat optional), and a baked or grilled marinated chicken. Make your own list of three dishes you can whip up at any time.

Holiday Decorating

I decorate sparsely for the holidays. I like decorations, but they can be a lot of work. Depending on the holiday and the type of decorations, many decorations can be classified as froufrou.

I always enjoyed handing out Halloween candy at my house even if it meant leaving work early to greet trick-or-treaters. I waited to write my evening emails to Europe after the last sign of trick-or-treaters.

When I had my own place, I was a minimalist when it came to Halloween decorations. My decorative efforts consisted of cutting a few pumpkins out of orange construction paper and taping them to the inside of the front window. That was enough to say, "Halloween is served here, and I'm handing out candy. Come and get it!"

At Christmas, I often visited family, so I skipped putting up a tree at my place. In a couple of my early bachelor years, I decorated with lights along the roofline of my house. Given the rough winters in the Chicago area, I hung lights on a warm day, around Thanksgiving. I took the lights down on a warm day after New Year's Day.

For those of you who haven't experienced a Chicago winter, a sunny day around Thanksgiving might be 45 degrees Fahrenheit. After New Year's Day, it might be a while before temperatures rise to the 40s. Factor in my motivation and the high probability of being at work on a relatively warm day, it might be March before my holiday lights came down.

After a couple years of decorating the roofline, I stopped putting up any lights on the house.

During a more recent Christmas, I felt especially motivated and decided to make my own fantastic holiday star—my sign of hope for a better future. Envision a beautiful star with shining, blue twinkle lights adorning a prominent tree in the front yard to convey the meaning of the season.

The Vision: The Star at Night

I decided to build my own perfect star as there wasn't anything like what I wanted available in stores.

I used five three-foot wooden dowels to build the frame of the star. Then, I took a string of blue LED miniature twinkle lights and attached them to the frame with twist ties. The initial test of the star while constructing it in the basement was a success; all the twinkle lights lit up.

During the day, I hung the star about ten feet up in a tree. After carefully routing an extension cord from the star to an electrical outlet outside the house, I tested the star. All the lights still lit up fine.

I couldn't wait to light it up that night. This would be the coolest star ever and homemade to boot!

The Reality: The Star at Night

That night, I saw the results of my handiwork and was

totally disappointed. I could barely make out that the lights were in the shape of a star.

With some imagination, I saw my creation had a vague star shape. It needed more lights.

I realized that doing more design work in advance, even for simple projects, is useful. That was the last year I tried outdoor decorations.

Minimalizing decorations saves the planet by using less stuff and the electricity used to run that stuff. Yes, I understand the sentiment and do enjoy seeing other people's decorations. It's tough…it's a trade-off, and each one of us needs to decide how to make that trade-off.

Apart from decorating, most of us use all kinds of stuff to make our lives easier and more pleasant. While we're using all this stuff, we can make some effort to make the stuff we use last longer and use as little energy as possible. By keeping stuff nice, it will last longer before it needs to be replaced. In the next chapter, I present some practices to help make your stuff last longer.

7

Keeping Stuff and the Planet Nice

I dislike unnecessary effort, especially when it comes to housekeeping. A bit of planning and upfront effort can ultimately save effort while also saving the planet. Win-win. Preventing things from getting dirty means those things don't need cleaning as often.

When you avoid unnecessary wear and tear on things, they stay nice and last longer before needing replacement. These are easy to obtain energy savings, and all these efforts help save the earth.

Here are some useful tips for keeping things nice while saving effort and energy.

Cleaning

There are two basic reasons things get dirty and need cleaning. First, an event happens like a food spill. Something clean becomes dirty instantly. Alternatively, things become dirty or dusty slowly—over days, weeks, or months.

It's best to clean up event messes quickly—preferably right when they happen; they only get harder to clean up as time passes. That spilled ice cream on the countertop can be wiped up with a stroke of a wet cloth right after the spill occurs. If you wait a few hours, the dried residue will take scrubbing and lots more water to dissolve the residue. After a few days, the surface and the ice cream remnants may seem permanently bonded together!

Always use a plate or spoon rest for cooking utensils while cooking. This keeps the countertop and stovetop clean.

For things that get dirty slowly, one tactic is to cover stuff with a washable surface. Lampshades often come covered with plastic to keep them clean during shipping and while in the store. I've left the plastic on lampshades to keep them dust-free for years. Make sure the plastic won't melt or catch fire when the lamp is on. You can also leave the light off or use a timer to save electricity.

I covered my couch with a large blanket to keep the

fabric clean. I often ate dinner sitting on the couch, resting my plate and glass on the coffee table. Using a place mat, a small towel, or even a magazine under the plate and glass kept the table clean and free from dreaded rings that glasses make on wood. I discovered putting a bath towel on the floor between the couch and the coffee table caught stray crumbs and the occasional drink, dip, or salsa spill. When the couch blanket or floor towel got too dirty, I threw it in the washing machine.

These practices saved countless carpet and upholstery cleanings. The carpet and upholstery cleaning necessitated by the Squirrel I incident was an exception to this effort-saving. Sometimes, you must dig in and clean.

Where it isn't practical to cover things with a washable surface, I give in and do some occasional dusting, sweeping the floor, vacuuming, and general cleaning of the bathroom. I do this cleaning a little at a time before things get too dirty. I've found I can dust very efficiently while having a phone conversation.

Clothing and Shoes

I've been experimenting with the khakis and jeans I wear to make them last longer. After years of observation, I noticed the very bottom of pant legs would start to fray while the rest of the pants were perfectly fine. To prevent this, I started folding the bottom of the pant legs up, forming a cuff and saving the bottoms from fraying and wear. I keep them cuffed mainly when I'm around the house or walking outside. I unfold the cuff when I'm headed into a business meeting or visiting someone.

Initial results are very good for both khakis and jeans. I've successfully prevented the bottom of the pant legs from fraying. However, on one pair of experimental khakis, the bottom of the pant legs looks new, but the fabric on the front of the thighs is starting to pill. This is my next area of pants research and experimentation.

After several years of practice and observation, I also developed the Sneaker Lifecycle.

I believe this is the best practice. For people who also wear sneakers for social occasions, this lifecycle works exceptionally well. The lifecycle requires that three or four pairs of sneakers be in circulation at any given time. That does seem like a lot of sneakers! However, follow the logic here; the goal is to maximize the life of each pair of sneakers.

First, consider the non-athlete or occasional sneaker-wearer. Start with a new pair of sneakers (see (1) on the Sneaker Lifecycle diagram). These sneakers are worn for social occasions, shopping, errands, and work (if applicable). Wear the shoes for these purposes until they start to smell or look bad.

Once a pair is no longer suitable for social occasions, wear them while doing dirty jobs (2). These jobs include cutting grass, cleaning the basement or garage, painting, or shoveling snow. This kind of wear takes a toll on the sneakers, and you don't want to subject your newest pair of sneakers to this treatment.

Eventually, the sneakers become filthy, worn, and broken down. They are no longer suitable even for messy jobs. At this point (3), use the sneakers for things like a canoe trip down a dirty river or camping. These activities will finish the useful life of the sneakers. Then, throw them out (4).

Athletes should start with a new pair of sneakers used for sport (see (A) on the diagram). Use this pair until the sneakers are too worn to use effectively for competition. How shoes break down under different sporting conditions varies widely. If the sneakers still look, feel, and smell good, and are okay to walk in, move them into circulation for social occasions (1). If the pair isn't good enough for social occasions, they move directly into use for messy jobs (2).

The frequency of how often new sneakers are put into circulation (1) or (A) and old pairs are discarded after going canoeing depends on your level of activity and frequency of canoeing. Once again, this may seem like many pairs of sneakers. But shoes stay newer longer when you follow this lifecycle. Fewer total pairs of sneakers are needed over many years, thereby maximizing the value derived from any given pair. Using fewer pairs of sneakers saves money and the environment.

Sneaker Lifecycle

(1) New Sneakers
Wear: social occasions, shopping, errands, etc.
start to smell, look bad/worn?
No
Yes
(2) Wear to cut grass or other messy jobs
totally dirty/worn?
No
yes
(3) Wear canoeing in dirty river
(4) throw out

(A) New Sneakers (Athlete)
Wear for your sport
too worn for sport?
No
yes
look okay, okay to walk in and smell okay?
Yes
No

©JWW 2019

Saving Energy (Pragmatic and Resourceful)

Early in my career, I worked as an energy-conservation engineer at a huge, energy-intensive plant. Part of my job was to identify leaking energy around the plant. I worked with maintenance people to eliminate the biggest energy leaks, such as steam leaking out of pipes and through equipment.

Once you become attuned to energy leaks, you realize leaks are everywhere. In a home or other building, common energy leaks are drafty doors and windows.

My plant experience led to the idea that I could save energy in my apartment by heating less of it. Saving energy can have a downside; if it gets too cold inside, water pipes might freeze in the winter. Frozen pipes cause enormous messes and repair bills, making any energy savings seem small.

Luckily, my apartment was well-suited for my energy-saving idea. The bathroom and kitchen were on interior walls (where all the water pipes were) and the bedroom and living room on exterior walls (no pipes).

To implement my plan, I hung clear plastic sheets from floor to ceiling, separating the kitchen and bathroom from the living room and bedroom. I also turned the thermostat down to 65 degrees and closed the heating registers in the living room and bedroom.

The kitchen and bathroom where the pipes and thermostat were located stayed warm. The rest of the apartment remained perceptibly cooler.

In retrospect, I'm not sure how much energy I saved because the apartment was in the temperate climate of Tennessee. However, the plastic sheeting in my apartment made an impression on other engineers who visited me. To this day, I'm not sure if the reaction was, "Oh, what a great idea," or "Oh, this guy is a nut!" but it was a fun experiment.

Replacing old thermostats with programmable models is a wise idea too. Why heat or cool your place beyond what is necessary to avoid problems when you're not home? Open windows and fans are useful during temperate months, and you'll save energy and money by using them when you can.

If you have drafty windows and doors, investigate readily available sealants, replace fittings, or rubber seals, or cover with weather-proofing plastic to eliminate the worst leaks.

Another easy way to save energy and gasoline is to plan your errands better. We've all heard of people driving five miles in one direction to a store, then driving five miles in the opposite direction to another place, and then driving back in the first direction again. This tip has been around for a while, but it bears repeating. Combining one's errands to cover a particular area of town, and planning in advance, can save a lot of driving (and your time). If you can afford it, you can also have groceries or meal kits delivered and free up a lot of time.

Use Less Stuff and Recycle

To do my part for the environment, I try to use less of everything—water, energy, paper, plastic bags, soap, cleansers, and packaged goods. I reuse and recycle stuff whenever possible. I'm fortunate to live where I can walk to the store if I don't have too much to carry. Individually and collectively, all these little things add up.

Anything wasted also wastes all the materials, energy, and labor it took to produce and transport items. Since environmental costs and limited resources are never fully accounted for in the prices of the things we consume, the price of something wasted is often not a good indicator of the size of the waste. It's essential that everyone does their part.

Surprisingly, many communities report most people don't recycle. This is an easy fix since most waste pick-up companies offer free recycling bins. If you are in an apartment, odds are there are separate receptacles for trash and recyclables. Make these work for you by installing two or three trash cans in your place (for paper, metal and glass, and waste). If your building doesn't offer recycling, call your landlord.

8

The Week from You-Know-Where (Making it Through Chaos)

There are times when we get over-the-top busy. If one or two unusual events occur, most of us can adjust to free up time and handle whatever needs to get done. When three or four extraordinary events occur, we can approach a breaking point. We might go over the edge into chaos.

One of those extraordinarily busy times happened to me when four unusual events piled up in one week.

Event #1: Trade Show

During this eventful week, I was scheduled to present the cool features of future telecommunications equipment at a trade show. A big plus was that the trade show was happening in nearby Chicago, and I was able to hop on the commuter train instead of flying out of town.

A week before the trade show, a coworker and I prepared slides for our presentation after hours in a conference room buried in the bowels of a large office building. At least we got that done ahead of time.

Monday night, before the trade show, I had to attend an evening orientation to learn the ins and outs of presenting at the show. At the orientation meeting, my coworkers and I also received spiffy new polo shirts to wear during the show.

The trade show set the tone for a busy week, though it wouldn't have been a big deal by itself. Like most things, it's when they pile up that trouble can quickly spiral out of control.

Event #2: Out-of-Town Choir Visit

When I was in high school, I was part of a church youth choir. The director was a wonderful minister who was kind to me during my awkward high school years. A couple months before the trade show, the minister called me unexpectedly and said his choir was visiting the Chicago area. He asked if I could find a church in the suburbs for the choir to perform. Also, could the church members provide places for the seventy-five choir members, parents, and staff to sleep? I couldn't turn down such a wonderful man and, having been on a few of these trips when I was in high school, I wanted to help. So, I said, "Yes. Of course, I can."

It took a few phone calls to find a church to host the performance. I started with churches of the same denomination. The music director from one church flatly refused, which surprised me. Another said yes, with one condition. It would be up to me to find people willing to host the choir members in their homes. In addition to providing a place to sleep for the night, the hosts would need to feed their choir guests breakfast the next morning and bring them to the church. From there, the group would catch their bus to start the next leg of their trip.

Finding hosts was an enormous task. Over the next few weeks, I made many phone calls to church members and friends. I became the master list keeper of willing hosts for all those souls and appreciated the people who stepped up to help. My goal was to find housing for everyone, but I ended up finding homes for only about fifty members of the group. This included four who would stay at my place, which was the maximum I could accommodate.

Up until a few days before the concert, I was still making

phone calls, looking for more hosts. Luckily, the minister's assistant for the choir group suggested that some of the group could stay at a hotel if I couldn't find housing for everyone.

Did I mention the concert fell on an evening in the middle of the telecom trade show? Throughout the process of finding the church and accommodations for all the members of the choir, my mind swirled.

Psychologists suggest that we have an ongoing dialogue with ourselves about how things are going in our lives. Some call this self-talk. My self-talk kicked into overdrive during this time. "I've got to be on the telecom trade show floor on Wednesday and Thursday. Seventy-five choir members are coming here on Wednesday night, and I'm responsible for housing them. Four of them are staying with me, and I'll be gone all day!" Yikes!

Event #3: Fixing Bathroom Tile

A couple weeks before the choir concert, knowing I was going to be hosting four choir members in my home, I decided to fix the loose ceramic tiles around my only bathtub and shower. I should have tagged this thought as insane, but I didn't. The tiles were a 1960s pink that might be considered retro and chic these days. Well, maybe not.

Fixing the tiles understates what I ended up doing. Like many jobs around the house, this repair job entailed a lot more than I realized at first glance. First, I assessed what was wrong by pulling a few loose tiles off. I discovered the wallboard behind the tile had degraded so much it had dissolved. A simple tile repair wasn't going to work.

My plan expanded to tearing out all the old tile and wallboard around the tub and shower. Then, I would replace the wallboard with waterproof concrete backerboard and install a beautiful new tub and shower surround. The composite shower surround was white and would glisten when installed. No more pink 1960s-era tiles and no more grout to clean. Yes!

Even though I started the tile project a couple weeks ahead of my visitors' arrival, it wasn't soon enough given the expanded scope of the bathroom project. Though I was busy at work getting ready for the trade show, I completed the demolition process of removing the old tile and wall the weekend before my guests were to arrive. Unfortunately, I hadn't begun installing the new concrete board and shower surround. Time was running out.

My inner dialog continued. "I've got to be on the telecom trade show floor on Wednesday and Thursday. Seventy-five choir members are coming here on Wednesday night, and I'm responsible for housing them. Four of them are staying with me. The only shower in my house has no walls."

In the few remaining evenings before the trade show and choir concert, I labored far into the night on the bathroom. I made progress, but the reality was beginning to set in—finishing this project in time for my visitors was unlikely. I installed the rough concrete backerboard but hadn't started on the shower surround when time ran out. The surround was supposed to be easy to install. But, of course, the shower surround wasn't exactly the right size and had to be precisely cut to fit the bathroom walls which weren't square like the beautiful, new shower surround.

On Tuesday evening, the night before the trade show and concert, I began to accept defeat. I wasn't sure how I could install the shower surround that night, so I took a break from the project. I needed to do a load of laundry. I turned my attention to the laundry while my mind percolated on what to do with the shower.

Event #4: Bad Dryer Smell

Essential life functions still need to occur regularly during busy times. Fast food, one-can meals, and peanuts come in handy to eat. As for laundry, I usually have enough clothes to make it through the week (see Laundry Management).

This week was an exception. I needed to do laundry. The spiffy new polo shirts with the corporate logo for the trade show required washing. I took a break from the bathroom project and threw the deep-red shirts in the washer with a load of color laundry.

When the wash cycle completed, I went to put the wet clothes in the dryer. "Whoooeeee," I exclaimed out loud, even though there wasn't anyone else in the house. "What's that smell?" Upon opening the dryer door, I smelled something terrible like ammonia mixed with other indescribably stinky odors. My eyes teared. Was it a dead animal? "Uggghhh!" What could have happened? I didn't know, and I didn't have time to find out.

I pondered the cute little chipmunks that frequented the area behind the house where the dryer vented. Maybe a chipmunk or another animal had decided to journey through the vent pipe into my dryer. Given the smell, I was confident that whatever was in the dryer was dead.

I began my search. There wasn't anything in the dryer drum. I tentatively turned the dryer on. It worked fine, but the intense smell would undoubtedly transfer to whatever clothes it dried.

My inner dialog continued. "I've got to be on the telecom trade show floor tomorrow and Thursday. Seventy-five choir members are coming here tomorrow night. Four of them are staying with me. The only shower in my house has unfinished walls. It's 9:00 PM. A chipmunk died in my dryer. My trade show shirts are wet, and I can't use the smelly drier because I can't go to the trade show in a shirt that smells like a dead chipmunk."

I considered my options. Taking the dryer apart—although I had done that a few times before—would take precious hours I didn't have. Who knew what would be inside the dryer? What would a chipmunk (or its remains) look like after being caught in the mechanical parts of a dryer? I could go to a laundromat and dry the shirts though this would be very time-consuming. The shirts might air dry by the morning, but they would be wrinkled. Who believes a telecom trade show presenter wearing a wrinkled shirt? Calling someone to take the dryer apart also crossed my mind, even at that late hour. There must be 24-hour help available in the vast metropolitan area.

I imagined the conversation if I called.

"ABC Appliance Repair. How can I help you?"

"Hello, do you repair clothes dryers?"

"Of course. We repair all kinds of appliances, including clothes dryers. What's up?"

"Well, my dryer smells like a small animal died somewhere inside it. I'm guessing it was a chipmunk due to the abundant population outside the dryer vent. Can you send someone to come find out what happened and fix it?"

"Buddy, are you over eighteen years old?"

"Yes. Why?"

"Well, you're old enough to take care of your own dead chipmunk. Deal with it, buddy!"

I eliminated the possibility of outside help, especially at this late hour.

Imagining what happened to ancient mummies, I arrived at a potential solution. Theoretically, the little dead creature in the dryer could be dried out. I decided to try running the dryer empty for an hour or more. Maybe the smell would go away.

I set the dryer timer for an hour. Safety note: running a drier when it's empty is not recommended by most dryer manufacturers. Check your make and model before trying anything similar.

With the dryer running, I turned my attention back to the bathroom project. The clock was ticking.

I had been using the living room floor as a staging area for the bathroom project. All the big, glossy-white, shower surround parts and plumbing components (tub spigot, associated knobs, and showerhead) were spread across the living room floor. The plumbing components were on an old sheet to keep the floor nice and clean.

I glanced through the booklet of shower-surround

installation instructions and started to think about the cuts I needed to make in the surround pieces to compensate for the crookedness of the walls. As with many do-it-yourself projects, instructions on how to handle unusual conditions like crooked walls were absent.

In a moment of clarity, I surrendered to the realization that there was no way I could install everything in the few hours I had left. And I needed to get some sleep so I could talk coherently at the trade show.

I needed another plan for the shower before my guests arrived. With time running out, I was desperate for a solution. What is the essence of an operational shower? I came up with three things.

1. Warm water falling over one's body

2. The water and soap suds draining away

3. The water and soap suds not permeating the walls or getting on the floor

I envisioned one of those showers seen in old black-and-white movies or in old mansions where the shower has been retrofitted onto a claw-foot bathtub. They used a shower curtain around the entire perimeter of the tub. Yes!

I made a quick run to a 24-hour megastore—one of those huge stores with everything from groceries to lawn tractors under one roof. My shopping list contained shower curtains, duct tape, and breakfast food for my guests. Before I left, I turned off the dryer and smelled inside. The smell had dissipated.

Upon arriving home, I checked the dryer again. The smell was gone. My experiment had worked! I dried my shirts while I hastily installed royal-blue shower curtains around the perimeter of the bathtub. I used copious amounts of duct tape to attach the curtains to the unfinished wall and punched holes in the plastic curtains for the showerhead and hot and cold water handles.

After I reinstalled the essential plumbing pieces, voila! I had a working shower.

I went further into recovery mode and took all the tools and shower-surround pieces from the living room to the basement. I quickly tidied up around the house, making my home look somewhat orderly.

It was a success, of a sort. My trade show shirts didn't smell like a dead chipmunk. I could take a shower, and so could my guests. Events had finally turned the corner. I went to bed around 3:00 AM.

Although I was sleep-deprived, everything went surprisingly well the next morning. I caught the train on time and got to the trade show without a hitch. I worked the exhibit with my colleague, explaining all the innovative features of the upcoming product.

The evening choir concert at the church went well. Everyone who had committed to hosting choir members showed up for their guests. I found the four people who were staying with me and drove them home. One of my guests was the wonderful minister I'd known in high school. On the way home, I mentioned my behind-schedule bathroom rehab work to reduce the potential surprise my guests would face when encountering my makeshift shower.

My guests understood the shower condition after hearing about the unexpected turns the project had taken. The minister even commented positively on my shower curtain handiwork, though to say he complimented my bathroom would be exaggerating.

After everyone was settled, I fell asleep in a sleeping bag on the floor of a spare bedroom I used as an office. Finally, peace.

The next morning, I brought my houseguests back to the church so they could catch their bus. I took the train back into Chicago for the final day of the trade show. On the train ride home, I fell asleep, exhausted. Fortunately, I woke up in time for my stop. My week from you-know-where had finally ended.

Taking Better Care of Myself

Although nothing disastrous happened during the week, since then, I've learned a lot about how I could have taken better care of myself physically and mentally. Instead of merely surviving the week, I could have enjoyed it. When living alone, there often isn't anyone around to have a moderating effect on your life. No one else might see that you're overly ambitious in what you're trying to accomplish and that you're not eating well or getting enough sleep.

From a planning perspective, I could have seen what was coming and decided not to be so ambitious with my goals.

Our society tends to reward and admire people who go overboard with their workload and personal commitments instead of taking care of themselves. I could have accepted that a few loose tiles in the bathroom would be okay for my guests and tackled the expanded bathroom project another time. In addition to enjoying the trade show and choir visiting experiences more, I could have gotten more sleep. Precious sleep.

There is an abundance of data showing reduced sleep severely impairs human functioning. The amount of sleep adults need for optimal functioning can vary, though I know three hours is not enough for me. Research shows most adults need at least seven or eight hours of sleep a night.

Dr. John J. Medina, a developmental molecular biologist, has researched and written a lot about how our brains function optimally. One area he researched involves sleep. Medina says sleep loss reduces executive function, attention, mood, quantitative skills, logical reasoning, working memory, and motor dexterity. We need these functions to be our best selves. Although the trade show and choir visit went well, I know I was not my best self.

What exactly is executive function? Executive function sounds like something reserved for executives in wood-paneled offices running large organizations—but it's not. Executive function is the ability to get tasks done. And getting multi-step, time-intensive tasks completed takes planning.

My planning was terrible during this period. Ouch, that hurts to write.

As I reflect on this period, I realize my inadequate sleep reduced my ability to plan. This lack of sleep led to a vicious downward spiral. I could have had a more positive outlook as I went through the week if I had been rested.

Since then, I've learned about a thinking technique called reappraisal. Sometimes, I have an overly negative view of life events, especially minor ones. Changing my thinking toward a more positive outlook, I could have chosen the following inner dialogue:

"My trade show presentation is ready, and it's great! Seventy-five choir members are coming here on Wednesday night, and I can't wait to hear them sing. They will be comfortable in the homes and hotel I've arranged. Four of them are staying with me, and it will be great to see the minister after all these years. My shower is torn apart, but I've figured out a temporary workaround. Something smells in my dryer, but I'll figure something out for that, too."

The above reappraisal isn't Pollyannaish. Work had to be done for the imperfect, yet operational solutions to all the problems I faced. The above reassessment is more optimistic. Using it, I would have been in a better mood while in the thick of it, and that better mood would have helped my problem-solving ability.

For sources about the power of reappraisal, see the reference section.

Positive thoughts reduce stress and improve performance. In his book *Leading Well from Within*, Daniel Friedland presents the Yerkes-Dodson Stress and Performance Curve developed by Robert Yerkes and John Dodson in the early 1900s. The inverted "U" shaped curve shows the relationship between stress (arousal) and performance. As shown in the figure, a certain amount of stress helps a person perform better. After passing the top of the curve, added stress decreases performance.

The Yerkes-Dodson Stress and Performance Curve

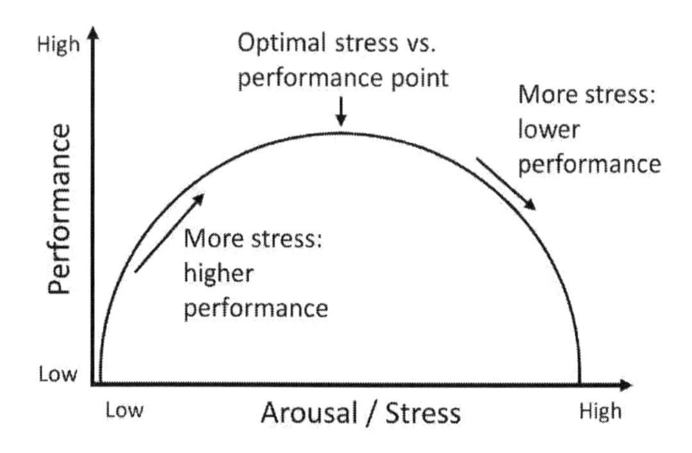

Adapted from "Leading Well from Within,"
by Daniel Friedland, MD

JWW 2019

Friedland's book also mentions another stress-response strategy I could have employed during this trying week—the "tend-and-befriend" response. Developed by Shelley Taylor, professor of social psychology at UCLA, the tend-and-befriend response is when we reach out to family, colleagues, and friends for collaboration and support. This takes away the loneliness of stressful situations and brings in more problem-solving ideas from others.

Although I reached out to others, asking them to host choir members, no one else had the big-picture view of everything I faced that week. I could have used help. Bringing others into my situation might have resulted in a suggestion to delay the bathroom rehab beyond that busy week. Using any of these tools could have made for a better experience.

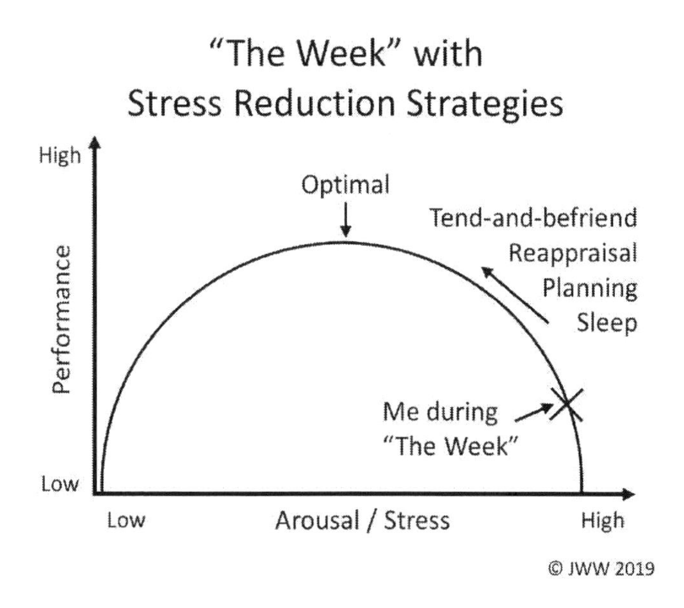

The figure above shows the Arousal/Stress curve applied to me and my week. Where I was operating during this week is marked with an X. With some stress reduction strategies and better planning, I could have operated from a more positive place, performed better, and had a better experience. When we are sleep deprived and stressed, our brain might not function well enough to remember these strategies and carry them out!

This leads to an important individual sustainability question—can you sustain the current pace of your life on a daily, weekly, or annual basis? If the answer is no, what can you do to make it better?

Finishing the Shower Rehab and the Dryer

Once the week ended, I had an ugly yet operational shower. I was physically and mentally exhausted from the shower project, the choir visit, and the trade show. I wish I could say I finished the shower project the next weekend, but I didn't. The shower was functional, so I decided to catch up on some sleep, which was more important than the project's completion.

I finished the shower project a couple months later at a slower pace.

The dryer continued to work without any smell.

A year later, the dryer needed a part replaced. Taking the dryer apart cautiously, I cringed at the thought of what I might find. What did I find? Nothing. No dried out little creature, no spatters of animal fluids, no other animal deposits. Nothing. What happened is still a mystery.

Revisiting the Cynefin Framework

Will the Cynefin framework help me make sense of this trying time?

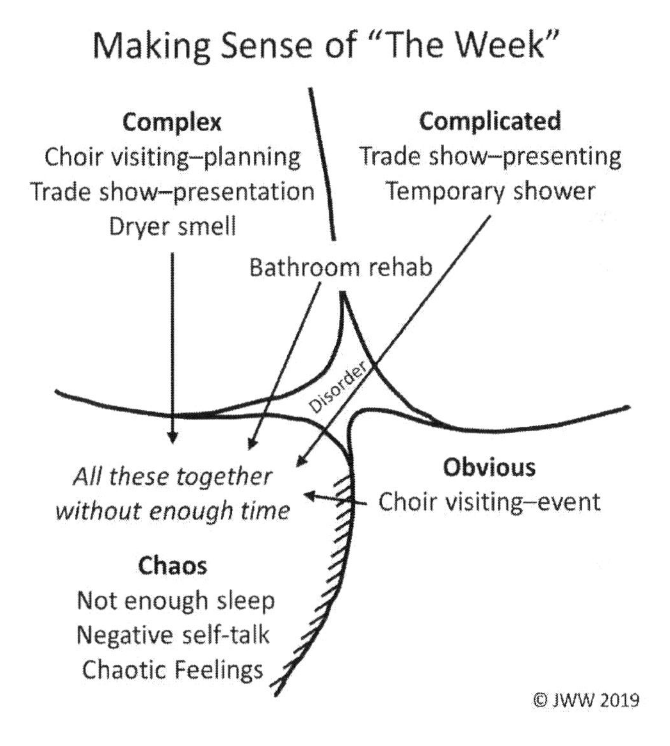

This is how I make sense of the different events. This analysis starts with the upper left of the diagram (complex) and works clockwise.

The planning part of the choir visit was complex, not because of the number of phone calls I had to make but because the response I would get to each call was unknown. Whether I was calling a church to find out if the choir could sing there or a potential host, each call was a small safe-to-fail experiment. I didn't know the outcome before I tried, or the number of calls it would take to accomplish my goals.

Working with my colleague to develop the trade show presentation was also complex. We spent many hours experimenting with various content on different slides, emphasizing different product features.

Figuring out the dryer smell was complex. I didn't know what was causing the odor, so I experimented with getting rid of the smell. My first attempt solved the problem, but if that hadn't worked, I would have had to do something else. Another experiment.

The bathroom rehab straddles complex and complicated. The complicated part involved several skills I developed over the years: carpentry, plumbing, reading complicated installation directions.

Complexity entered the bathroom rehab when the directions for the shower surround didn't cover the circumstances of my bathroom (crooked walls).

Presenting at the trade show was complicated. My colleague and I had to be experts on the future telecommunications product to give a good presentation. We also had to answer questions from potential customers who saw our presentation.

The temporary shower enclosure I created was complicated; some amount of design was needed along with expertise in using duct tape. Maybe this kind of skill is bordering on the obvious. I also used plumbing skills so water could flow into the temporary shower.

From my perspective, the actual event of the choir visiting was obvious. At that point, everything had been planned, and it was a matter of carrying out the plans. I literally just showed up a half-hour before the concert. By concert time, people had been assigned to hosts or the hotel. After the concert, people went to their assigned places, and it all happened without a hitch. Note: this is from my perspective. The choir's performance was complicated to them—the choir used their singing expertise.

Why was this week so trying then? Everything I've described was complex, complicated, and obvious. A lot of the work was also done in advance. The chaotic feelings and sense of disorder I had were due to lack of sleep. I didn't have enough time to do everything; I over-committed myself. Negative self-talk also contributed to my sense of chaos and disorder.

To partially recover, I gave up on the bathroom being finished for my guests. Another thing I've learned when facing these kinds of overcommitted situations is to keep moving toward meeting the multiple goals in front of me. Doing the most vital things first becomes super important.

The Cynefin framework helped me make sense of this time. If I'm ever faced with a similar situation when there is too much going on, I can make better choices by not overcommitting myself. I can also focus on getting enough sleep. If I had done this, the experience would have been more enjoyable for me. You can use the Cynefin framework to make your life feel easier too.

Trivia question: How many shower curtains does it take to completely enclose a bathtub on all four sides? Answer: Three.

9

Visitors

As evidenced by the choir members who stayed with me, visitors can pose a problem to the bachelor household. Although most people don't expect a squeaky clean and orderly place when entering bachelordom, the state of my kitchen might have shocked visitors. Revealing exactly how I lived could have caused some embarrassment.

Once, when a guy friend unexpectedly stopped by, I said, "Oh no, someone must have broken in! Look, they've completely ransacked the place!" Of course, he saw through my little story.

There are three things to consider when thinking about visitors. One is how much you care about what other people think of your housekeeping. Second is how much of the house your visitor will see. Third, the amount of advance notice you have before visitors arrive will determine what you can do to put your best foot forward.

If you don't care what your visitors think of your housekeeping, it's easy. Just go with the flow.

If you care and have some time, clean up the things that will embarrass you the most. If you're following the system from earlier in the book, load the dirty dishes in the dishwasher. Fold up the blanket kept on the couch and put the towel you use to catch spills between the sofa and the coffee table into the laundry. Be sure the bathroom is clean. If you have an extra bedroom where the visitors won't go, stash as much as you can in there. A closet with any amount of space can also be used to stash stuff. If you're in the middle of a project (like redoing your bathroom or working on your car's drive shaft in the living room), finish the project or at least put the parts out of sight. Or develop a fantastic story to impress your guests with your industriousness.

If you care deeply about what your guests might think, you're going need some time in advance of their visit. In addition to doing everything in the above paragraph, engage in some major clutter reduction. Put all the food on your kitchen countertops away in the cabinets. Clean out your refrigerator. Refer to the earlier section on cleaning.

Hopefully, you've kept up on some of the cleaning to-do items all along.

You never know when a totally unexpected visitor my show up, so you might want to come up with a plan for this situation too.

One early summer morning, I was working from home before going to the office. I needed to make a few phone calls to leave messages for my coworkers. In the office, there was five-digit dialing between phone extensions. Because I was working, my mind acted as if I were in the office. To reach one coworker, I dialed 91135 from my home phone. Shortly after dialing, I realized I wasn't at work, so I hung up. I dialed the full number and left a message. I called the next colleague at 91187. Oops! I'd made the same mistake again. I hung up quickly.

I've got to wake up, I thought.

I called the second colleague's full number and left a message. With my homework completed, I went to my bedroom to get dressed before heading into the office.

A few minutes later, my doorbell rang, and I heard loud knocking on my house's side door. Who was there? Hardly anyone ever showed up unexpectedly, especially at this time of the morning. I quickly pulled on some pants and a t-shirt and went to the door, barefoot.

A police officer greeted me. She wore a microphone

pinned to her dark-blue shirt, a gun, and she had a black, wooden club hanging from her belt. I'm not sure what expression I had on my face, but surprise wouldn't fully capture it.

The police officer kept some distance from the door. "Sir, is everything all right in there?"

"Yes," I said, perplexed.

"Do you live alone?"

"Yes. Why? What's wrong?"

"We've had several 911 hang-up calls from here."

It dawned on me that mistakenly dialing the five-digit numbers to my coworkers had not been benign. I had accidentally placed calls to 911 and hung up. The police officer thought some trouble or who knows what might be going on in my house. Someone might need some help. Oh man.

I explained how I had dialed 911 by accident while trying five-digit dialing when working from home.

The condition of my home ran through my mind. Dirty dishes piled on top of the dishwasher. Canned goods and cereal boxes on the countertops. Books everywhere. Clean, unwrinkled shirts hanging everywhere. The officer would see all of this when she entered the side door that led into the kitchen. What would she think? Luckily, there's not a law against lousy housekeeping.

"Would you like to come in and look around?" I asked as confidently as I could.

The officer looked at me sideways and said, "No, that's okay." She grabbed her microphone and relayed some coded message to her dispatcher.

My story must have been believable, or she was afraid to come into my house—not fearful of me but afraid of seeing my bachelor household.

10

Cynefin and Lean: Putting it all Together

As I've philosophized about all the goings-on at my home, at my work, with lean, and with the Cynefin framework, I've come up with some insights.

The next diagram combines lean dimensions with the Cynefin framework. This helped me make better sense of my personal life, my work, and the world in general.

In the obvious area, outcomes are predictable. In these situations, it's possible to strive for lean—that is, doing things in a way that has high resource efficiency and high time efficiency. After some practice, I can get my laundry done quickly with a minimum of labor and resources such as water, soap, and electricity.

In the complicated area, experts are needed to do the work. Only the work of experts can result in predictable outcomes. Lean is possible, but only by the experts. Many of us attempt easier repairs around the house, but it takes us a long time because we're not experts. Thus, with plumbing, it might take me four hours to change a faucet, while a plumber could do it in one hour.

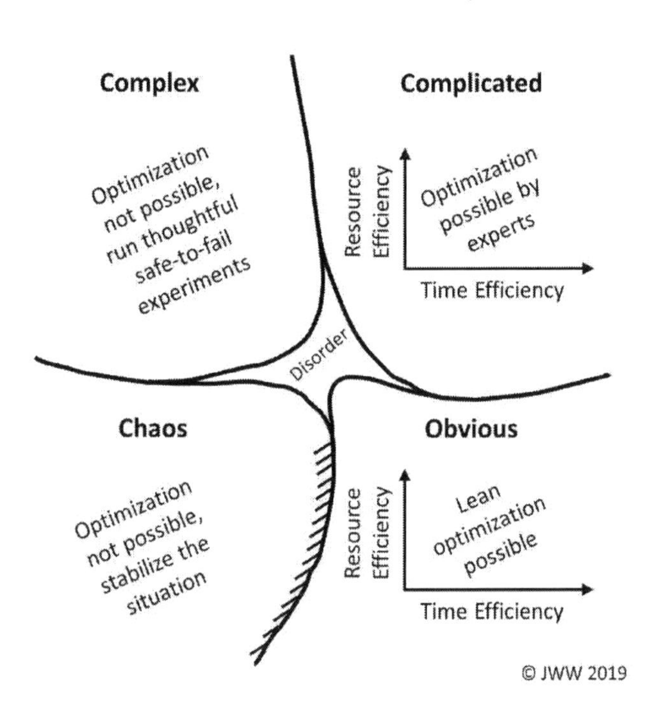

When it comes to the complex area, lean isn't possible

because no one knows for sure what's going to happen as a result of a certain set of actions. The best one can hope for is efficiency of experimentation when doing safe-to-fail experiments that have a chance of succeeding. Most times, some expertise is needed in the field of experimentation.

In chaos, outcomes are totally unpredictable. All one can do is act to stabilize the situation.

After internalizing the framework, I've come to some other conclusions.

- To someone who isn't an expert in a field, something complicated will seem complex or even chaotic.

- Experts in a field may see a complex situation as complicated if they don't grasp the true complexity of the problem. Difficult interdisciplinary problems are usually complex.

- Even though work is obvious doesn't mean everyone can do it; the right skills and equipment may be required.

- When work is done by teams, discussion about which domain the problem is in is useful.

Disagreement is especially helpful because conflict means the problem and potential solution isn't understood the same way by everyone.

- It's challenging to apply lean solutions—that is, solutions that are resource and time-efficient—to anything but obvious problems. It may be possible to apply lean solutions to complicated issues that have been sufficiently narrowed, so answers are obvious to those who work on the problems.

- Chaos can ensue if enough time and resources are not available to handle a situation.

- Problems and situations involving people are often complex.

Here, I humbly offer a view of the world mapped onto the Cynefin framework.

Cynefin and the World
Selected Observations

Complex
People
Human development
Some relationships
Management
Leadership
Organizations
Technology development
Economics, Investing
Environment
Many world problems

Complicated
Repeatable design
Great manufacturing
Great service delivery
Some relationships

Disorder

Chaos
Natural disasters
War
Riots
Some relationships

Obvious
Some transactional relationships

Everyday stuff

Collectively, we face a boatload of complex and complicated problems. How can we all make it better?

Epilogue

I hope you've enjoyed taking this journey with me, that you've had a few laughs, and learned a few things as I've recovered some of my artistic path.

I'm no longer a bachelor and am happily married.

My 1950s ranch house was very solidly built but existed in a neighborhood where the land became more valuable than the house. After I got married and moved out, I sold the house. Soon after, it was torn down—even though it had a relatively new roof and a spiffy shower surround. It was time for me and the house to move on.

Lauren, my wonderful wife, saved me from myself and many of my bachelor practices. In our household, the dishwasher gets emptied after it's run, and the dishes get put away properly in the cabinets. Dirty dishes don't get stacked on top of the countertop. I've kept some of my optimized-value way of doing laundry, but the clothes generally get put away and hung up. I'm not always fishing through the clean laundry basket for socks and underwear.

We've not had any squirrels in the house, but when unusual situations present themselves, I now have a trusted partner and friend to help me figure out how to handle the complicated and complex situations. She's great at helping me when I need the tend-and-befriend method of stress reduction. She suggests I go to sleep when I might stay up working on a project.

Life is better.

I hope you've learned a few things that will make your life around the house a little better too, and I wish you happiness and success.

Thank You

I want to thank the following people for their help and contributions to this book. I thank Dave Snowden for his permission to use the Cynefin framework; Niklas Modig and Pär Åhlström for letting me use their lean model; and Daniel Friedland for the Yerkes-Dodson curve and other information from his book. Thanks to Michele and Ken Budka at Full Sail Publishing for their wonderful job editing this material and making suggestions to make this book better. And finally, thanks to my wife, Lauren, for offering constant encouragement during the writing process.

References and Notes

Chapter Two

Lean:

Modig, Niklas, and Pär Åhlström. *This is Lean: Resolving the Efficiency Paradox*. Rheologica Publishing, 2012.

Note: In their book, Modig and Åhlström use flow efficiency instead of time efficiency for the x-axis of their lean diagram. See their book for their full description.

Chapter Three

What people spend their time on:

"American Time Use Survey 2017 Results." U.S. Department of Labor, Bureau of Labor Statistics, June 28, 2018. https://www.bls.gov/news.release/archives/atus_06282018.pdf.

Kanban:

Skarin, Mattias. *Real-World Kanban: Do Less, Accomplish More with Lean Thinking*. The Pragmatic Programmers, LLC, 2015.

Chapter Four

References on the Cynefin framework:

Snowden, Dave. *The Cynefin Framework*. Conwy, UK: Cognitive Edge, 2010.

CognitiveEdge. "The Cynefin Framework." YouTube. YouTube, July 11, 2010. https://www.youtube.com/watch?v=N7oz366X0-8.

"Cynefin framework." Wikipedia: The Free Encyclopedia. Wikimedia Foundation, July 2004 https://en.wikipedia.org/wiki/Cynefin_framework.

Snowden, David J., and Mary E. Boone. "A Leader's Framework for Decision Making." Harvard Business Review, November 2007. https://hbr.org/2007/11/a-leaders-framework-for-decision-making

Chapter Eight

The importance of sleep:

Medina, John. "Sleep: Brain Rules." Brain Rules. Accessed February 7, 2019. http://www.brainrules.net/sleep (text and video).

Medina, John. "About Author John Medina: Brain Rules." Brain Rules. Accessed May 27, 2019. http://brainrules.net/about-the-author.

Note: Medina also has a book titled *Brain Rules* published by Pear Press in Seattle, WA.

Reappraisal:

Tan, Chade-Meng., and Colin Goh. Pages 201, 202, and 203 in *Joy on Demand: The Art of Discovering Happiness from Within*. HarperOne, an imprint of HarperCollins Publishers, 2016.

Webb Caroline. Pages 261-264 in *How to Have a Good Day: Harness the Power of Behavioral Science to Transform Your Working Life*. New York, NY: Crown Business, 2016.

Friedland, Daniel, MD. Pages 102, 103, and 144-152 in *Leading Well from Within: A Neuroscience and Mindfulness-Based Framework for Conscious Leadership*. San Diego, CA: SuperSmartHealth, 2016.

The Yerkes-Dodson Stress and Performance Curve:

Friedland, Daniel, MD. Page 97 in *Leading Well from Within: A Neuroscience and Mindfulness-Based Framework for Conscious Leadership*. San Diego, CA: SuperSmartHealth, 2016.

The tend-and-befriend response to stress:

Friedland, Daniel, MD. Page 58 in *Leading Well from Within: A Neuroscience and Mindfulness-Based Framework for Conscious Leadership*. San Diego, CA: SuperSmartHealth, 2016.

Executive Functioning:

"Executive functions." Wikipedia. Wikimedia Foundation, July 22, 2004.
https://en.wikipedia.org/wiki/Executive_functions.

About the Author

Jim Weihrouch \ "Why-Rock" \ has always been curious about how things work. Though he earned bachelor's and master's degrees in engineering, he wishes he'd learned about lean practices and the difference between solving complex and complicated problems earlier in his career as an engineer and project manager. This is Jim's second book; his first was *Joy at Work*. Jim lives in a suburb of Chicago with his family. Connect with him on LinkedIn.

Made in the USA
Columbia, SC
01 November 2019

82380812R00093